Elizabeth

FORTUNE'S BASTARD?

ABOUT THE AUTHOR

Richard Rex is Director of Studies in History at Queens' College, Cambridge. He has written and researched extensively on Tudor England and his other books include *The Tudors* (also published by Tempus), *Henry VIII & the English Reformation* and *The Lollards*. He lives in Cambridge.

RICHARD REX

TEMPUS

This edition first published 2007

Tempus Publishing Limited
The Mill, Brimscombe Port,
Stroud, Gloucestershire, GL5 2QG
www.tempus-publishing.com

© Richard Rex 2003, 2007

The right of Richard Rex to be identified as the Author
of this work has been asserted in accordance with the
Copyrights, Designs and Patents Act 1988.

British Library Cataloguing in Publication Data.
A catalogue record for this book is available from the British Library.

ISBN 978 07524 4176 4

Typesetting and origination by Tempus Publishing Limited
Printed and bound in Great Britain

Contents

	Preface	7
1	Birth: 1533	13
2	Early Years: 1534–1553	19
3	Elizabeth and Mary: 1553–1558	35
4	Accession: 1558	49
5	The Alteration of Religion: 1559	59
6	Scotland and the Succession: 1559–1568	81
7	Mary Queen of Scots and the Catholic Problem: 1568–1580	107
8	War with Spain: 1580–1588	183
9	The Earl of Essex: 1589–1601	199
10	Death: 1603	213
	Further Reading	217
	List of Illustrations	221
	Index	227

In memory of the hundreds of northern men
hanged under martial law in January 1570

PREFACE

The fourth centenary of the death of Queen Elizabeth I will probably fill a shelf with biographies and studies, old and new – not to mention publications in other media. What possible justification can there be for adding to them? Only the hope of catering to part of the demand for information about a monarch who inspires perennial interest. This contribution will be not the biggest on the shelf. If it is to have any claim to distinction, it may perhaps be as the shortest book on Elizabeth published in 2003. If you want something more informative and interpretative than an article in an encyclopaedia, yet shorter and sharper than a full-scale biography – a sprint rather than a marathon – this is for you.

The dedication calls for some explanation. Last year, Queen Elizabeth fought off fierce competition to secure a place in the BBC's 'Top Ten Great Britons'. Sadly for her admirers, the eloquent and enthusiastic advocacy of the Rt Hon. Michael Portillo was not enough to bring her overall victory in the contest. The main plank in his platform was Elizabeth's place as the fountain-head of the English tradition of tolerance. There is much truth in this happy picture. Elizabeth was no religious fanatic. As she reportedly said, she had no desire to 'open windows into men's souls'. And the English tradition of tolerance and fairness, though not unblemished, is something we should honour, cherish, and hand on unimpaired to future generations. Yet we should not put on the rose-tinted spectacles when we look at that tradition. Even as Mr Portillo praised Elizabeth for preserving England from the horrors of religious conflict and persecution experienced elsewhere in Europe, the pictures chosen to illustrate those horrors gave the game away. The graphic depictions of men being executed and dismembered were as 'real' as any such pictures can be. But they showed neither the atrocities of the French Wars of Religion nor the victims of the Spanish Inquisition. Taken from a broadsheet published at Rome in 1555, the pictures showed the execution of Catholic monks in

London under Henry VIII in the 1530s. Far from being spared such scenes, Elizabeth's England was to see Catholic priests hanged, drawn and quartered not merely in London but in many other towns throughout the 1580s and '90s.

It was this irony, and the implied contrast with Queen Mary, in whose short reign 300 Protestants were burned for heresy, which induced me to look in more detail into a fact which rarely appears in the biographies and histories of Elizabeth, namely that in the reprisals after the rising of the northern earls in 1569, some 900 men were executed. Frankly, I suspected that the figure might be exaggerated, as such figures often are. Indeed, a case has been made for reducing the tally of victims to a 'mere' 450, although it smacks of special pleading. Yet even at that level, these reprisals would remain the cruellest episode in the history of Tudor England. And the documents in the case point towards the higher figure.

The Earl of Sussex dealt with Durham, selecting 200 victims from the county in addition to about 100 others, mostly clergymen, ringleaders and close associates of the rebel earls, who were executed in the city. We have a detailed list, village by village, township by township, allocating the 200 victims according to the level of participation of each place. He then ordered Sir

George Bowes, a northern knight who had held out against the rebels at Barnard Castle and was subsequently entrusted with the administration of martial law in the region, to execute 200 men each from the three other areas which had taken part in the rebellion: Richmondshire and the bordering parts of the North and West Ridings of Yorkshire. Sir George carried out his task with the grim satisfaction of a man whose lands and houses in the region had been systematically pillaged and trashed by the rebels. His brusque summary of his efforts in 'sifting of these rebels' reports 'six hundred and odd' executions. All within two or three weeks, without trial, under martial law. Some of the designated victims may have escaped execution, but the sources give us no reason to believe that there were very many lucky ones. As Sir George laconically remarked, the hangings had left 'the people in marvellous fear'.

Apologists or bigots may argue endlessly about the relative merits of execution for heresy and treason in Tudor England. Traitors or martyrs, the victims were just as dead. Those hundreds of men had doubtless joined the rebellion for a host of different reasons. Perhaps in the end they were just a few of the myriad 'fools of Time, which die for goodness, who have lived for crime'. But the driving force behind their crime was their resentment at a government which had taken their religion away. Their main achievement was to restore the altar in Durham Cathedral and to hear once more the old Latin Mass. The rebellion itself collapsed with little more than a siege and a skirmish. There were far more deaths in the reprisals than in action. And although this rebellion was one of the least threatening in the history of Tudor England, it was punished with unparalleled savagery. Was Elizabeth to blame? She could have shown mercy, but she did not. Her only intervention, it seems, was her 'special commandment' not to select victims from the ranks of freeholders or those who were reckoned at all wealthy. It was not even justice, let alone toleration or – a virtue which was valued in the sixteenth century – mercy. So the dedication is just a little exercise in truth and memory, which must rank among the foremost objectives of the pursuit of history.

I
BIRTH: 1533

If my dear love were but the child of state,
It might for Fortune's bastard be unfathered...

(Shakespeare, Sonnet CXXIV)

Elizabeth Tudor was born about 3 o'clock in
the afternoon of Sunday 7 September 1533. The
birth was a devastating blow to her parents.
She was meant to be a boy. The astrologers and
physicians and midwives had promised it. God
owed it to the papally appointed Defender of the
Faith and self-appointed Supreme Head of the
Church of England. Anne Boleyn, Henry VIII's

second wife, the woman for whom he had thrown over a marriage and a church, had failed. The grand tournament with which Henry had been planning to mark the birth never took place. Eustace Chapuys (Emperor Charles V's ambassador), who was Catherine of Aragon's staunchest supporter in England, was gleeful at Anne's discomfiture. It was not the end of the affair. But it was a bad start.

Catherine of Aragon, Henry's first wife, had in one way done better than Anne. For her first child had been a boy, Prince Henry. But his death after just a few weeks – which has as good a claim as anything to have been a turning point in English history – set the pattern. Few of her pregnancies came to term, and only one of her children, Mary Tudor, survived infancy. Had Prince Henry survived, Henry VIII would never have felt the need to question the legitimacy of his marriage to his late brother's wife; Anne Boleyn might have been just another of the king's amours; and Elizabeth might never have been born at all – at least, not born to the purple. But Catherine had failed to produce the son the king needed and desired. With the passing years she had lost her appeal for the king, and, more to the point, her fertility. In the later 1520s, Henry began to entertain doubts about the legitimacy of his marriage to Catherine, doubts which rested on the fact that she had originally been married to his elder brother Arthur (whose death in 1502 was another of those many turning points).

It all came out into the open in 1527, when Henry began sounding out his councillors and scholars about whether the pope was really in a position to allow a man to marry his brother's widow – which seemed to breach the biblical prohibition against marrying a brother's wife. There were intellectual problems: the Bible also contained a commandment enjoining marriage to a childless brother's widow. And there were political problems: Catherine was the aunt of the most powerful prince in Europe, the Holy Roman Emperor Charles V; and he in turn was in complete control of Italy and of Rome, effectively tying the hands of the pope, who was the only man who could sort out Henry's matrimonial difficulties. At home, sympathy for Catherine as the wronged woman mixed with healthy contempt for Anne, the 'goggle-eyed whore', as a home-wrecker. Yet Henry wore down and beat down opposition at home, secured French diplomatic support abroad, and gradually lost faith not only in the papacy's willingness to give him what he wanted, but also in its very legitimacy as the central authority of Christianity upon earth.

The path to a solution began to clear in 1532, when the ageing and intransigent Archbishop of Canterbury, William Warham, finally died. There had been no prospect of this dour old cleric sanctioning any unilateral solution to the crisis, of the kind which Henry's advisers had by now concluded was required. But Henry, quite possibly acting on Anne's recommendation, chose as his successor Thomas Cranmer, a man who had been working for the divorce as a scholar and a diplomat for several years, and could therefore be relied upon. A summit meeting with the King of France was arranged, and Anne Boleyn, made Marchioness of Pembroke in her own right, was invited to join the royal party. Sure that marriage to the king was on the cards, she seems at last to have surrendered her body to him during that cross-Channel excursion, which lasted from mid-October to mid-November. If Anne did not actually conceive during that trip, then she certainly did so shortly afterwards, as she knew by Christmas that she was pregnant.

Anne was understandably pleased with herself once she became aware of her condition, and some hasty marriage ceremony seems to have been arranged, although it was highly secret and cannot be dated with any certainty. Cranmer's return to England in January 1533 allowed formal proceedings for the annulment of Henry's first marriage to begin. By the time these formalities reached their foregone conclusion at Dunstable in May, Anne's condition was public knowledge. It was unmistakable to those who turned out, over the Whitsun weekend, to witness the festivities in London which marked her coronation as queen on 1 June. (According to Chapuys, her reception was at best muted, if not downright chilly. But he was a far from unbiased reporter.) It was not long before Anne retreated into the privacy of the royal palace at Greenwich to prepare for the birth of her son. But the son turned out to be a daughter.

Henry put as brave a face as he could upon the disappointment. Official letters announcing the birth were sent far and wide. The christening of the baby, on 10 September, was a splendid occasion. It was held in the church of the Observant Franciscans which was in effect part of the palace complex at Greenwich. The Duke of Norfolk was Anne Boleyn's uncle, and his stepmother the Dowager Duchess, matriarch of the vast Howard clan, stood godmother (as she had also done for Mary back in 1516), entrusted with the task of carrying the child to the font. Thomas Cranmer was godfather, and the Bishop of London, John Stokesley, performed the ceremony. The church was packed with Boleyns, Howards, and their many family connections.

II

EARLY YEARS: 1534-1553

A household was soon established for the young Princess Elizabeth, initially at Hatfield in Hertfordshire, but as mobile as all royal households. Mary, demoted from a princess to a mere ladyship, and stripped of her own household, was sent to serve in that of Elizabeth, though she refused to acknowledge her own demotion or to yield any service to her infant rival, despite the abuse and ill-treatment meted out to her on Queen Anne's instructions. Mary's deep-rooted hatred of her younger sister is not hard to understand.

Over the winter, the king's chief minister, Thomas Cromwell, worked on an Act of

Succession which would put the legal position of the principal characters in the drama beyond all possible doubt. Elizabeth was to be recognised as heir presumptive, pending the birth of the son whom Anne was still confidently expected to bring forth. The act became law in March 1534, and an oath to its contents was to be tendered to every adult male in the kingdom, starting at Court. In order to show his personal investment in the act and the oath, Henry summoned Elizabeth to Court at Eltham, and made a very public show of his favour and affection for her as the oath began to be more widely administered. The oath was sworn by all but a handful of the London clergy to whom it was offered on Friday 17 April. An even clearer message went out the following Monday, when the oath was offered to the citizens of London. One of the leading public opponents of Henry's divorce, a nun from Canterbury named Elizabeth Barton (the 'Holy Maid of Kent'), was executed that morning with some of her supporters.

Princess Elizabeth spent the next few years in the relative seclusion of her own household, except when Henry felt the need to reiterate his commitment to the new order. Thus, when Catherine of Aragon died in early 1536, Elizabeth was paraded in a display of bravado as Henry himself ostentatiously donned a garish yellow outfit to celebrate his first wife's death. But within a few months, Anne Boleyn's reputation was in tatters, as her own indiscreet words and behaviour fuelled suspicions in Henry's mind that she had committed adultery and even incest. Elizabeth last saw her mother from a window in Greenwich Palace, as Anne was led away to be taken to the Tower of London. Not yet three years of age, she would have had some idea of what was going on, but it is unlikely that she retained much memory of that day, or of her mother, in later life. Anne was executed on 19 May, shortly after Archbishop Cranmer had annulled her marriage to Henry. A second Act of Succession, passed in June, excluded Elizabeth, like Mary before her, from the succession, which was now entailed upon the offspring of Henry's third wife, Jane Seymour. Elizabeth, like Mary before her, had been declared a bastard – potentially a shattering experience in such an honour-bound culture as Tudor England, though less so at just under three years of age than at sixteen. This dénouement came as a particular joy to the imperial ambassador, Chapuys, whose despatches had since Elizabeth's birth persistently referred to her, with deliberate disdain, as 'the bastard'.

But royal bastards were a special case. Royalty went a long way to removing the taint of

illegitimacy in the blood of those whose father-
hood was acknowledged – and Henry could
hardly disown Elizabeth. Although Elizabeth
spent little time at Court, that was the usual fate
of royal children after infancy and until their
teens. In the later 1530s, she resided mostly in
the Home Counties, along with her elder sister
Mary, who had been reconciled to her father
in summer 1536, after the death of her own
mother and the execution of Elizabeth's had
deprived her of her main moral support and her
chief grudge against Henry. In these years the
king's daughters are found variously at Hatfield,
Havering, Hertford Castle, Hunsdon, and elsewhere. Mary was more often at Court than
her sister, especially during the brief reign of
Queen Jane Seymour, but Elizabeth too made
some visits, as in March 1538, when she and her
young brother, Edward, were staying a few miles
from Hampton Court for the benefit of foreign
ambassadors.

Ironically, Elizabeth was the beneficiary of a
social change introduced into English aristocratic culture by two of the people who were
least happy to see her come into the world
– Catherine of Aragon and Sir Thomas More.
Thomas More, implementing in his own household at least one of the ideals laid out in his
vision of Utopia, had given his daughters the

kind of formal education hitherto reserved for boys – indeed, his daughters seem to have been brighter than his son. Catherine of Aragon had induced another of the leading humanist scholars of the 1520s, Juan Luis Vives, to compile for the benefit of Mary a handbook setting out a programme for an up-to-date female education. In due course a talented humanist scholar, Richard Fetherstone, was hired as her tutor. Elizabeth, like her sister before her, was to benefit from as good an education as the sixteenth century could provide. Her French tutor was John Belmayn, who also taught Prince Edward. Certainly Elizabeth's command of French was impressive. Her translation of Marguerite of Navarre's *Mirror of the Sinful Soul,* which she presented to Catherine Parr as a New Year's gift in 1545, was a feat which would be testing for today's English students of French at sixth-form or even university level. The mildly evangelical tone of the work chosen for translation was itself consonant with the tastes of Belmayn, who in the later 1540s set Edward VI to compose a bitterly antipapal treatise in French. Italian was also on Elizabeth's early curriculum, and a letter to Catherine Parr in Italian is one of her earliest surviving compositions.

Once she moved on to Latin, Elizabeth studied successively under two graduates of St

John's College, Cambridge, then the foremost scholarly institution in the land – incidentally benefiting from the labours of yet another of her mother's bitterest enemies. John Fisher, Bishop of Rochester, who was largely responsible for making St John's such a centre for modern scholarship, had also been the chief among those who defended the validity of Henry VIII's marriage to Catherine of Aragon. First under William Grindal and then Roger Ascham, Elizabeth became a gifted Latinist and competent in Greek. In a well-known letter to a foreign educationalist, Johannes Sturm, Ascham could find no better means of praise than to compare her to the daughters of Thomas More – whom, of course, she excelled. Many years afterwards, Ascham put forward Elizabeth as living proof of the pedagogical methods he advocated in his handbook, *The Scholemaster*. According to him, Elizabeth,

> by this double translating of Demosthenes and Isocrates daily without missing every forenoon, and likewise some part of Tully [i.e., Cicero] every afternoon, for the space of a year or two, hath attained to such a perfect understanding in both the tongues, and to such a ready utterance of the Latin, and that with such a judgement, as they

be few in number in both the universities,
or elsewhere in England, that be, in both
tongues, comparable with Her Majesty.

If the genuinely stylish Latin oration which,
after a suitable display of maidenly modesty,
she delivered before the duly astonished masters and students of Cambridge University in
summer 1564 really was delivered on the spur
of the moment in something like the form in
which it survives (hastily transcribed by one of
those present), then it shows that she had indeed
attained the ultimate objective of a humanist
education: to produce a person who could
deliver extempore orations ('ready utterance')
in elegant Latin. Elizabeth retained a lifelong
taste for the classics, and Ascham's praise for her
attainments was not all flattery. She translated a
variety of classical texts for her own diversion
and edification, including Seneca, Cicero and
Horace. It was as much to the consolations of
philosophy as those of religion that she turned
in adversity, and in 1593 she translated Boethius's
Consolation of Philosophy, that least dogmatic of
Christian writings.

Elizabeth's main political value in the latter
years of Henry's reign was as a counter on the
diplomatic gaming-table. From the improb-
ably early age which was customary among

royalty, possible marriages were mooted for her. Potential husbands included princes from France, the Holy Roman Empire, Piedmont, Denmark and Spain. But the uncertainty which Henry's kaleidoscopic matrimonial career had created regarding the legitimacy of his daughters and the inheritance of his throne was a recurrent obstacle to the progress of these plans. Such plans, of course, were often at best half serious, and never for a moment gave any consideration at all to the preferences or happiness of Elizabeth herself. Early in her own reign, she told a foreign ambassador that her father had once toyed with the idea of marrying her to the Scotsman James Hamilton, Earl of Arran, himself a bastard, and that while she herself had been far from keen on the match, she knew that if it had been her father's will, she would have had no choice.

It was in the 1540s that the young Elizabeth began to appear on the public stage in her own right. She and Mary were among the noble ladies sent to greet Anne of Cleves upon her arrival in England early in 1540, and they were at Greenwich in summer 1543, among the witnesses to their father's sixth and final marriage, to Catherine Parr. Mary was more and more at Court in the 1540s, and was to join Catherine Parr's household, while Elizabeth, still a child, tended to be lodged away from Court with the young Prince Edward. But towards the end of the reign, she too was spending more time at Court. This increasing public acceptance of the two sisters was sealed in Henry VIII's third Act of Succession, passed early in 1544. Mary and Elizabeth were both restored to the line of succession, respectively second and third after Edward. Under their father's will, which confirmed their rights of succession, they were also each to be endowed with lands worth about £3,000 a year, as well as substantial cash dowries in the event of marriage. Their rehabilitation was virtually complete. Only the taint of illegitimacy remained to cast a shadow over their matrimonial prospects.

Elizabeth was residing at Enfield when she heard of her father's death. The news was broken to her by Edward Seymour, Earl of Hertford, who was on his way back from Hertford to London with his nephew, the young Edward VI, to whom he broke the news at the same time. As Elizabeth was not yet old enough to preside over her own household, she lived at first in that of her stepmother, Catherine Parr. There she became prey to the affections and ambitions of Sir Thomas Seymour, Lord Admiral of England and the younger brother of Edward Seymour, who, as uncle to the young king, had smartly seized power – making himself Duke of Somerset and Lord Protector of the Realm. Sir Thomas, hoping to rival his brother's success, had briefly dreamed of marrying Elizabeth before settling for the late king's widow, securing Catherine's hand in marriage with what most people saw as indecent haste. Catherine, who had borne no children to Henry, was pregnant by the end of the year, and as a result Thomas's interest in Elizabeth seems to have reawakened (sexual intercourse during pregnancy was reckoned harmful to the unborn child according to the medical opinion of the time). His visits to her room first thing in the morning, clad in his nightshirt, literally for a bit of slap and tickle, were seen by Victorian historians as shockingly immoral and by mid-twentieth-century historians as innocent frolics. Today 'the mattier of the admirall' tends to be seen as somewhere between sexual harassment and child abuse. The sixteenth century was no more sentimental than our own about the likely path of relationships between middle-aged men and teenage girls, and the scandal was soon brought to the attention of Seymour's wife. Her first solution – to join in the fun, thus ensuring by her presence that things could not go too far – was at best an unhappy compromise, and she seems to have realised this. In summer 1548 Elizabeth left the

Seymours, and before the year was out she had a household of her own, under the tutelage of a governess, Katherine Ashley, and a 'cofferer' (financial manager), Thomas Parry. Both Ashley and Parry were to remain her loyal servants for the rest of their days.

Catherine Parr gave birth in September, but died from the complications attendant upon the delivery. Thomas Seymour was once more free to marry, and his thoughts turned immediately to Elizabeth, now of a marriageable age. Mrs Ashley was all too keen to press his claims upon her ward, but Elizabeth, characteristically, responded with caution. Her often recorded denials of interest in Seymour have been interpreted as mere coquetry, and her teenage blushes at Mrs Ashley's unsubtle hints about his intentions have been seen as a sign of real affection. Such signs can easily be misinterpreted, and Elizabeth has left us no direct evidence of her feelings about her suitor. Rumour, however, was as clear about her willingness as about Seymour's plans, which horrified the rest of Edward VI's government, from the Duke of Somerset down. Early in 1549, Seymour was arrested on a variety of charges of treason, including his plan to marry Elizabeth. Her household was temporarily broken up as her closest confidante, Katherine Ashley, and her chief adviser, Thomas Parry, were both whisked away to the Tower for interrogation on the details of Seymour's intrigues. Elizabeth too was interrogated. Although she was spared the Tower, the Council sent Sir Robert Tyrwhitt to investigate her part in events. Yet although he was sure that she knew far more than she would say, he never broke her down.

In this, the first real test of her life, Elizabeth began to develop the technique that was to serve her so well throughout her life, counter-attacking and seeking to throw her opponent (or partner) off balance. Her theme throughout this episode was that her reputation was being defamed by popular rumours about her alleged relationship with Seymour, and that it was the government's duty to issue a proclamation against such rumours and those who peddled them. Although no trace of it survives, this may have been done in some form, as another of her letters to Somerset thanks him and the Council for issuing such a proclamation.

Somerset's time, however, was running out. Since the start of the reign he had been pursuing a decisively Protestant religious policy, in consultation with Thomas Cranmer. Summer 1549 saw this policy culminate in the abolition of the old Latin Mass and its replacement by a new English liturgy, set out in the first Book of Common Prayer. Together with economic hardship, this sparked off widespread riot and rebellion across southern and central England, from the West Country to East Anglia. In the wake of these rebellions, the other members of the Privy Council strove to reassert its collective authority, as under the terms of Henry VIII's will, against Protector Somerset, whom they believed to have provoked the crisis through his arrogance and to have prolonged it through his indecisiveness. Somerset's enemies were keen to get both Mary and Elizabeth on side, and wrote to them carefully explaining their position. But neither Mary nor Elizabeth played any part in the complex manoeuvres of autumn 1549, which saw Somerset displaced by a new regime led by John Dudley, Earl of Warwick.

Like Mary, Elizabeth evidently had real affection for Edward, whom they had both known since he was a baby. Both of them bestowed the customary New Year's gifts upon him. Mary had enjoyed a warm relationship with Edward's mother, Jane. They were much of an age, and shared an essentially traditional Catholic piety. As well as being old enough to be his mother, Mary doubtless derived some satisfaction from the way that Edward, whose legitimacy none could question, definitively dislodged Elizabeth from the succession. A Catholic source written many years later alleged on eyewitness testimony that the young prince had taken especial pleasure in Mary's company. But even if this can be trusted (and the account, a life of Mary's confidante Jane Dormer, is clearly in error on many points), it may mean little more than that Mary could afford better presents. While from the mid-1540s we have copybook letters to his sisters expressing copybook affection for them, it is hard to find evidence that Edward reciprocated his sisters' feelings after he came to the throne. Indeed, he lost all patience with Mary as her attachment to the Mass became ever more intransigent, and ever more unacceptable to the teenage zealot. Elizabeth is barely mentioned in the journal which Edward kept, and never with any sign of affection; and while Mary figures frequently, she does so only as the object of his disapproval.

While Edward was still a boy, the vital political connections were with those around him – and with those around them. In 1549 Elizabeth began to forge links with a rising star of English politics, William Cecil, a gifted Cambridge graduate who was becoming ever more influential as, in effect, private secretary to the Duke of Somerset. After giving an audience to the Venetian ambassador in September, Elizabeth had Thomas Parry send Cecil a report of the meeting as 'she will know or do nothing which seems important without his [the Protector's] understanding'. In the wake of the Seymour affair and then the risings of 1549, her caution was quite proper. Luckily for her, Cecil survived the fall of his first master and rapidly attached himself to the new dominant male at Westminster, the Earl of Warwick. Elizabeth kept in touch. In 1550 the lands which were rightfully hers under her father's will were at last made over to her as she approached adulthood, and it was probably in this context that she shrewdly appointed William Cecil as her surveyor (in our terms, her estate manager) – even more shrewdly allowing him to appoint a deputy to discharge his duties, leaving him merely to draw a handy fee. It may have been her connection with Cecil, and his influence with Warwick, that lay behind her successful bid to offer some of her lands to the Earl of Warwick in exchange for the royal manor of Hatfield, which now was to become her principal residence until her accession.

III

ELIZABETH AND MARY:
1553-1558

It was to be John Dudley, by this time Duke of Northumberland, who posed one of the biggest threats to Elizabeth's prospects of eventually occupying the English throne. For, as Edward VI lay dying in spring 1553, Northumberland encouraged the young king to attempt to alter the succession in order to prevent the Protestant Reformation from being undone by Mary Tudor, then next in line. Although religion was obviously the motive for the attempt, it was not an acceptable reason. A pretext was therefore sought in Mary's illegitimacy under English law, which could plausibly be said to debar her from inheritance. Unfortunately for Elizabeth, this argument militated as strongly against her claims as against Mary's. Edward VI's hopes therefore focused upon the third in line for the throne, Lady Jane Grey, the eldest granddaughter of Henry VIII's younger sister, Mary. (Henry VIII's will, which enjoyed statutory force thanks to the third Act of Succession of 1544, had passed over the Stuart line, descended from his elder sister, Margaret, in favour of the Grey line.) It was no coincidence that Jane was married to Guildford Dudley, one of Northumberland's sons.

In the event, Mary Tudor reacted to this intrigue with unexpected vigour. As soon as she was certain of Edward's death, she headed for her landed estates in East Anglia and summoned the nobility and gentry to support her claim to the throne. Mary's support snowballed while Northumberland's melted away, and she achieved a bloodless victory. This first crisis of Mary's reign left Elizabeth safe enough. She was not Northumberland's main target in summer 1553, and therefore played a characteristic waiting game, gathering her own supporters at Hatfield. Once it was clear which way the wind was blowing, she gave every indication of endorsing her sister's claim to the throne. Self-interest dictated her policy, for Mary's claim rested on the same basis as her own, the Act of Succession of 1544. It is unlikely that Elizabeth could have outmanoeuvred Northumberland if Mary had failed to overcome him. It was her good fortune that Mary, in vindicating her own claim to the throne, also safeguarded Elizabeth's.

After Northumberland's surrender, the two sisters entered London together in August 1553, and Elizabeth for a while enjoyed a place second only to the queen at Court. As the Venetian ambassador noted, Mary at first treated her younger sister with every sign of respect. However, her first parliament regularised the legal uncertainties over the queen's own legitimacy, recognising Henry VIII's first marriage to Catherine of Aragon, and in consequence condemning his union with Anne Boleyn as bigamous, and its offspring, Elizabeth, as a bastard. Now Mary had no further need of her support, and with the gulf of legitimacy between them spelled out, she spurned her sister with all the Tudor contempt of the true born for the base born.

Mary's religious policy did not put Elizabeth in any immediate danger. Mary immediately set about restoring the Mass and the sacramental and ecclesiastical system of Roman Catholicism, but it was not until January 1555 that heresy once more became a criminal offence liable to the death penalty. And in any case Elizabeth had long since conformed to the Mass. Although one wonders whether anyone other than Mary was fooled, she made an increasingly open display of Catholic piety. According to Jane Dormer, it was Elizabeth's practice in Mary's reign to hear two Masses a day and to show extraordinary devotion to the Blessed Virgin Mary. However, we should be careful in interpreting Elizabeth's frequently recorded protestation, 'I am a Catholic', reiterated right at the end of Mary's reign for the benefit of agents sent by the queen. While 'Catholic' generally meant and still means 'Roman Catholic', it was just as possible then as now for a sincere Protestant to claim to hold the 'Catholic' faith. Elizabeth could be as economical with her truth as she was with her money.

The second crisis of the reign, provoked chiefly by Mary's decision to marry a foreign prince (Philip of Spain), but partly also by her determination to restore Roman Catholicism in its fullness, put Elizabeth in a far more difficult position. When a group of aristocratic and predominantly Protestant conspirators, including Sir James Croft, Sir Thomas Wyatt, Sir Peter Carew and the Duke of Suffolk (Jane Grey's father), began to plot against Mary, it was inevitable that their attention would focus on Elizabeth, the heiress presumptive and from their point of view a safer religious bet. A marriage between Elizabeth and Edward Courtenay, Earl of Devon (who had been the leading English contender for Mary's hand) was their plan for securing the succession, and Elizabeth's known Protestant sympathies encouraged some of the conspirators to consider using her to displace Mary from the throne, and to try to involve her directly in the plot. If Elizabeth was perhaps drawn in some of the way (the evidence is far from clear), then it would have been precisely because a marriage between Mary and Philip might still have produced children and thus ended all hope that she herself might attain the throne in due course.

After picking up some rumours and leaks about the plot, Mary's Lord Chancellor, Stephen Gardiner, brought in Courtenay for questioning and induced him to reveal all he knew. The conspirators had to move prematurely, and as a result it was only in the traditionally volatile county of Kent that a rebel force was raised, led by Sir Thomas Wyatt. On 25 January he published a manifesto whose stated aim was to prevent Mary from marrying Philip, and he marched on London. Despite the relatively small numbers of his troops, Wyatt came close to success. Many of Mary's advisers panicked and advised flight. However, stirred by a courageous speech from Mary herself, which anticipated the performance of Elizabeth years later at Tilbury, the Londoners barred their gates against Wyatt. He was unable to force London Bridge on 3 February, and it took him a few days to make his way round via the next crossing, at Kingston. His assault soon crumbled, and he was captured.

The day after Wyatt declared his intentions, Elizabeth had been invited by the queen to join her in London for her own safety. Countering with a plea of ill-health, Elizabeth had demurred, and Mary sent her own physicians to assess her condition. But it was with Wyatt's capture that Elizabeth's troubles really began. The following day, Charles V's ambassador, Simon Renard, was commenting on the Duke of Suffolk's confession of the plan to put Elizabeth on the throne, and on 10 February Mary's agents personally presented Elizabeth with a royal summons to London. However, they reported the physicians' view that the princess really was ill, and recommended that she be allowed to make her way to London by suitably easy stages. She eventually arrived on Friday 23 February, to be lodged at first in the queen's palace of Whitehall (away from the river, as she had asked, for the sake of her health).

It was widely believed that Elizabeth was in grave peril. Her father would never have spared anyone on whose behalf such a rising had been attempted. There were those about the queen who thought that Mary could never be secure until Elizabeth was in her grave. Foremost among them was Simon Renard, who had enormous influence with the queen as the spokesman of her powerful cousin and of her intended husband, and was tireless in advancing the argument. However, neither Mary nor Elizabeth after her inherited the instinctive ruthlessness of their father, nor did they proceed against their enemies by means of the 'act of attainder', the parliamentary shortcut past the tiresome formalities of judicial process to which he had so often resorted. So the interrogations of Wyatt and the rest concentrated on the search for evidence against Elizabeth. But while it was clear that the plot had been undertaken in her interest, and even that attempts had been made to draw her into it, no incontrovertible evidence of her involvement was forthcoming. Moreover, there was a strong party among Mary's councillors, led by Lord Chancellor Gardiner, which was strangely anxious to preserve the life of Edward Courtenay – who certainly had waded far enough into the plot to make his execution a real possibility. A crucial letter implicating

Elizabeth went astray – according to Renard, because Gardiner feared that it would destroy Courtenay as well. Yet again, when her fate was entirely out of her own hands, Elizabeth was saved by a stroke of good fortune.

Nevertheless, when in the midst of these investigations Elizabeth was taken from Whitehall to the Tower, she feared the worst. In fact, although its symbolic overtones could hardly be overlooked, the move was more a matter of convenience than a threat. At that moment the government was planning to call a parliament at Oxford instead of at Westminster, as was by now customary, and to transfer the Court there for the duration. Ultimately, these plans came to nothing, but in the meantime there was simply nowhere other than the Tower in which anyone felt that the princess could be held securely during the queen's absence. The Earl of Sussex came to supervise the move, and Elizabeth characteristically went on the counter-offensive. She prevailed upon him to allow her, contrary to his instructions, to write a letter to the queen – a gambit which caused them to miss the tide and thus won her a day's respite, although it did not win her the personal interview with the queen which she had sought. On Palm Sunday 1554 she was therefore taken downstream to the Tower while the London crowds were at

High Mass in their parishes. Her protests availed nothing, and she was locked up for weeks.

Hoping to extort a confession where they had been unable to secure testimony, the Privy Council, led by Gardiner, came as a body to intimidate and interrogate her. But Elizabeth refused to be overawed, and kept her nerve. The longer she held out, and the further the memory of the imminent danger of early February faded, the more her friends around the queen were able to lobby on her behalf. Having got Elizabeth into this mess, it was Wyatt who finally got her out of it. He chivalrously used his customary privilege of speech at the scaffold, on 11 April, to exonerate her from all complicity in the rebellion – much to the annoyance of those presiding over his execution. Testimony such as this, uttered as it was by someone expected and expecting imminently to meet his maker, was commonly credited with almost gospel truth. The political difficulty of shedding royal blood in the teeth of such notorious and authoritative testimony was overwhelming. Popular opinion in London, already sympathetic to the princess, now became vocal on the subject of her innocence. Within a few days Elizabeth was free to take the air in the Tower gardens.

A month later, on 19 May, she was released from the Tower. Popular rejoicing, however, was premature, for she was not set at liberty. Nor was she allowed anywhere near the queen. On the contrary, she was taken, via Richmond, Windsor and High Wycombe, to Woodstock, where she remained for almost a year in the custody of Sir Henry Bedingfield, a loyal Norfolk gentleman who had been among the first of those who rallied to Mary's bid for the throne in summer 1553. Sir Henry, a man of stout heart but limited talents, was ill-equipped for what he must have quickly realised was one of the least enviable jobs in England. Painfully aware that Elizabeth might one day become his sovereign, he was clearly overawed by the superior status and wit of his prisoner. She pestered him endlessly, pushing relentlessly against whatever limits were placed upon her freedom of action. She was careful, of course, to conform to the requirements of the Catholic faith, and to ensure that Bedingfield duly reported her conformity to the Council – even if some of her own servants were less accommodating. Early on she teasingly asked to borrow his English Bible, and must have anticipated his uncomfortable reply, that he had never had one. But she kept up the pressure until she was allowed a copy. She made him constantly aware that she resented her confinement, demanding books and letters, manoeuvring him into acting as her secretary, and rapidly achieving a complete moral ascendancy over him. Sensitive from the outset to the status of 'this great Lady', he was soon addressing the Council as if he was more her servant than Queen Mary's: she had 'willed and required' him to forward a request of hers to the Council, and 'commanded' him to bring her writing materials. It is not surprising that Bedingfield yearned for relief from his duties.

What brought his release, and Elizabeth's, was Mary's presumed pregnancy. For in April 1555, Mary summoned Elizabeth to Court to witness the birth of the expected child that summer, delighted at the prospect of rubbing her sister's nose in her personal triumph. But the long summer at Hampton Court saw no royal birth. Fortune had turned the tables, and the triumph was Elizabeth's. Perhaps the sudden collapse of her hopes sapped Mary's will, or else the sight of Elizabeth's demure religious conformity at Court made her sister seem less of a threat. Either way, after that disastrous summer, Elizabeth was not put back under house arrest but was allowed to withdraw to her manor at Hatfield, where she resumed a quiet existence with such old friends as Katherine Ashley. The occasional plots which rippled the surface of politics over the next few years inevitably found recruits among the more hot-headed of Elizabeth's servants and connections. But Elizabeth herself, unlike Mary Queen of Scots later on, was too shrewd to be sucked in with them. If she had perhaps dipped her toes in the Wyatt conspiracy, she had learned her lesson now. After all, there was no more need for her to take risks. In the wake of the fiasco of 1555, Mary's chances of a child looked remote – the more so as her husband had now left the country. All Elizabeth had to do was wait: a policy which would serve her well through the years. She had nothing to gain from participating in harebrained ventures. A successful plot would have put her on the throne even if she did not take an active part, while involvement in a failed plot might have brought her to the block.

The wait proved shorter than Elizabeth might have expected. Catherine of Aragon had reached fifty, and Henry VIII had reached fifty-five, but Mary was to die a few months short of her forty-third birthday. Philip's brief second visit to England in 1557, which secured English involvement in his war with France (setting off the chain of events which resulted in the loss of Calais early in 1558), left Mary once again under the misapprehension that she was pregnant – although this time, in contrast to the first occasion, her confidence was not widely shared. As the due date came and went once

again, in spring 1558, the symptoms of her sup-
posed pregnancy turned imperceptibly into the
symptoms of her final illness. Eventually, Mary
was prevailed upon to accept the inevitable by
recognising Elizabeth as her heir. She voiced
the vain hope that Elizabeth would preserve her
religious settlement. Sir William Cecil, who had
also been waiting, had already emerged from
retirement to take his place at Elizabeth's side,
to prepare for the smoothest transfer of power
in the Tudor era.

IV

ACCESSION: 1558

Mary Tudor died early in the morning of Thursday 17 November 1558. According to Jane Dormer, who was with her, she died peacefully. Her final hours saw her fitfully dreaming of the children she had yearned for in vain, and her last conscious act was to behold the elevation of the body of Christ in the celebration of the Mass. The deaths of her three Tudor predecessors (Henry VII in 1509, Henry VIII in 1547, and Edward VI in 1553) had all been kept secret for days as the Court tried in each case to manage the transition to its own advantage. There was no such secrecy this time. Mary's Council proclaimed Elizabeth within a few hours, and messengers set off immediately to notify Elizabeth at Hatfield. It all went like clock-work. It might have been different. Had King Philip been at his wife's side, he might perhaps have been tempted, notwithstanding the provisions of his marriage treaty, to grasp at the reins of power (which is not to say he would have succeeded). But he was in the Netherlands. At Hatfield, Elizabeth set to work with the nucleus of her Privy Council, and under Cecil's experienced guidance the machinery of the new government started to turn at once. The formal records of the new Privy Council commence a couple of days later, on 20 November, and early public business was handled with impressive despatch. The Provost of King's College, Cambridge, had died a few days before Mary, and on 13 November the college had written to Mary for advice on the election of a replacement. On 19 November they sent a similar letter to the new queen, adding some timely congratulations. They got a response by return of post: a letter from the queen dated 21 November, recommending the merits of a certain Dr Philip Baker, whom they duly elected. A few days later, Elizabeth set off for London, making her ceremonial entry, amidst popular rejoicing, on Monday 28 November, the day after the first Sunday in Advent.

Her arrival heralded a prolonged festive season. In contrast to the quiet and decorum at the Court of the prematurely ageing Mary, Elizabeth's Court was filled from the start with youthful effervescence. Festivities continued through the twelve days of Christmas, and culminated in the queen's coronation on Sunday 15 January 1559. However, the coronation itself heightened some of the tensions which had already been arising over the central issue of Tudor politics: religion. The queen's Protestant preferences were no secret, and Mary's Catholic bishops were unwilling to lend Elizabeth the almost sacramental sanction of ritual anointing and crowning. This could have been deeply embarrassing, but the Bishop of Carlisle was prevailed upon to perform the ceremony in the absence of any of his more distinguished colleagues. But the air remained electric. The service was held, as usual, in Westminster Abbey, to which Mary had restored the monks in 1556. Elizabeth brusquely ordered the monks to take away their candles, assuring them that she had enough light to see by. And as the Bishop of Carlisle would not obey Elizabeth's command to omit the elevation of the Blessed Sacrament in the Mass, the coronation Mass had to be celebrated by the Dean of the Chapel Royal. Nevertheless, these moments of friction did not detract from the popular celebrations outside the abbey.

Elizabeth's accession was neither as theoretically improbable as her grandfather's nor as practically troublesome as her sister's, but it was not without its curiosities and potential problems. As the daughter of Anne Boleyn, born while Henry VIII's first wife, Catherine of Aragon, was still living, Elizabeth was illegitimate under the Catholic canon law which Mary had restored in England. If that was not enough, she was also strictly speaking illegitimate under the law of the land. The vicissitudes of Henry VIII's succession laws had seen Elizabeth first in line for the throne under the first Act of Succession (1534), then bastardised and displaced by the second act (1536), before being restored as third in line for the throne under the third act in 1544.

However, the massive repeal of Henry's laws which had taken place under Mary had left Elizabeth in a legal limbo from which there was no escape. Elizabeth could hardly pass an act retrospectively remedying this mess without acknowledging that she was illegitimate, which would have implied that she could not lawfully have taken the throne in the first place. This dilemma, while constitutionally amusing, was not of great moment, and was passed over in tactful silence. Fortune's bastard, though unfathered in her turn, came to the throne without fuss. In the event, Elizabeth's accession was domestically

untroubled, as the arrival of a young and probably fertile queen offered the realm new hope
in the gloom which had overwhelmed Mary's
last year. Mary's final illness gave both Elizabeth
and the English elites ample time to prepare for
the transition. The loss of Calais, the epidemic of
influenza, and the phantom pregnancies which
were all the fruit of her unpopular marriage
with Philip II had dissipated the stock of popular support which had swept Mary to power five
years before.

However welcome Elizabeth may have been
domestically, there were also foreign interests to
be taken into account, primarily those of her
cousin Mary Queen of Scots, whose legitimacy
none could call into doubt, and who was married to the Dauphin of France (soon to become
King Francis II). Although formally excluded
from the throne by Henry VIII's legislation, in
terms of blood and lineage Mary Stuart certainly had the best claim after Elizabeth. Indeed,
doubts about Elizabeth's legitimacy might have
provided Mary – or to be precise the powerful
and numerous aristocratic dynasty of the Guise,
her cousins, who dominated her and her young
husband – with a pretext for launching a rival
claim to the English crown. The natural anxieties
of the Elizabethan regime were hardly assuaged
when the young princely couple started to

quarter the English arms with those of France in their heraldic emblems. Elizabeth's ambassador at the French court, Nicholas Throckmorton, was instructed to deplore this in no uncertain terms, and Elizabeth herself took the gesture as a personal insult as well as a political threat. Her moral ground was perhaps not quite as strong as it might have been, given that she, like all her predecessors since Edward III, quartered the fleur-de-lys of France with the lions of England in her coat of arms, and claimed the crown of France as part of her formal title. But the English claim to France had been heavily discounted through over two centuries of conflict, whereas the French claim to England was an unsettling new move on the diplomatic chessboard.

The ominous attitudes struck by France, however, were counterbalanced by Philip II of Spain, who, now he was rid of a wife for whom he had never felt great affection, briefly entertained the possibility of prolonging his short reign as King of England by marrying his deceased wife's sister – whom he had always found more attractive. There was never much prospect of this, as the marriage would have been the mirror image of that between Henry and Catherine of Aragon, on the intrinsically incestuous character of which rested Elizabeth's own claims to legitimacy. His polite offer was equally politely refused. Despite the disturbing direction of Elizabeth's religious policy, though, Philip was especially anxious to maintain good relations with England during the peace negotiations following the cessation of the recent war with France. And he could not afford to let Elizabeth's right to the throne be called into question, as this might open England to the prospect of a Stuart succession and an alliance with France. Following his example, Catholic Europe therefore recognised Elizabeth.

The accession of a new queen of very different background and attitudes from her predecessor inevitably meant changes at the heart of government, on the Privy Council. It was the end of the road for those who owed their places on the Council to their role in placing Mary on the throne. Elizabeth, like Mary before her, brought her own personal retinue to the Council, such as her loyal servant Sir Thomas Parry, and her cousins Sir Francis Knollys and Sir Richard Sackville. That retinue also provided her most important appointment: her Secretary, William Cecil, who had been surveyor of Elizabeth's lands since 1550. Too closely implicated in the Edwardine regime ever to get far under Mary (though he had done occasional public service in her reign), he had looked to the rising star of Elizabeth for some time. Cecil brought his own network of kinship and friendship into her service. His brother-in-law, Nicholas Bacon, was given custody of the Great Seal as Lord Keeper. And the clergy who were called upon to advise on religious questions, and were soon to be promoted to the high places in the new church, were often drawn from the circles in which Cecil had moved in his youth at Cambridge, particularly from his own college, St John's. It is well known that many of Elizabeth's councillors were connections of the extended Boleyn family. Even Thomas Parry, for example, was married to the widow of Sir Adrian Fortescue, one of Anne Boleyn's many cousins, and that family in turn provided her in later years with Sir John Fortescue and Sir Thomas Bromley. The vast Howard clan, which provided still more of her servants (most notably Howard of Effingham), was also part of that family network. Yet this should not lead to suspicions of unthinking nepotism. Providing for relatives, if one was able to do so, was on the contrary considered a moral obligation at that time. And none of those relatives whom Elizabeth selected for high office disgraced it. The Boleyn and Cecil kin-groups were reasonably talented, and Elizabeth seems to have inherited her father's gift for talent-spotting.

Throughout her reign, though, there was another line of courtiers and officials who owed their careers not to their family or other prior connections with the queen or Cecil, but to their enjoyment of the queen's special favour. The Earl of Leicester (Robert Dudley), Sir Christopher Hatton, the Earl of Essex (Robert Devereux) and Sir Walter Raleigh all won that favour initially through their personality or their figure rather than through useful service. Double standards inevitably affect the historical judgement here. When a king's roving eye fell upon shapely young women at court, the implications might include another royal bastard and perhaps even some dividends in land and office for the young lady's family, but only rarely did it redraw the political map. On those occasions when a royal mistress had intervened in politics, she had inevitably aroused fierce resentment (as, for example, Alice Ferrers had done in the declining years of Edward III). Thus for a gentlewoman to catch the king's eye might mean personal advancement, but was not an obvious channel for political ambition. For an able young gentleman, catching the eye of the unmarried queen was a much more obvious path for ambition. Elizabeth should not so much be criticised for recruiting some of her closest political advisers this way as congratulated for choosing from the throng of those fighting for her attention only those that were worth promoting. The

Earl of Oxford, a worthless wallflower, made no political impact despite the initial appeal which he had for the queen. He was certainly one of the most colourful personalities of the age. But a deep vein of instability flawed his character. From the curious episode of his youth in Cecil's household – when an unfortunate cook was deemed by a coroner's jury to have committed suicide by running upon the earl's sword! – to his short-lived conversion to Roman Catholicism, his ill-fated marriage to Cecil's daughter, and his scandalous affair with the nymphomaniac Ann Vavasour (one of Elizabeth's Maids of the Bedchamber), his career was an object lesson in political failure. If the later favourites, Raleigh and Essex, were less stable than Leicester and Hatton, no one could doubt their abilities: it was simply that their ambition over-reached them.

V

THE ALTERATION OF RELIGION: 1559

The first business of the new reign was the settlement of religion – or the 'alteration of religion' as it was rather more aptly described at the time. Back in the reign of Edward VI, Stephen Gardiner had protested against swift religious change on the grounds that the Bishop of Rome 'wanteth not wits to beat into other princes' ears that where his authority is abolished, there shall, at every change of governors, be change in religion'. Edward's and Mary's reigns had both vindicated his warning, and Elizabeth's reign virtually turned it into a political principle. When James I came to the throne, the idea that religion changed with each new monarch was stated as a matter of fact. In the case of Elizabeth, there was no doubt about the direction of change. The only question was how far and how fast it would go.

Elizabeth's own religion has always been something of an enigma. In a secular age, she has at times been seen as an essentially secular person, her Christianity merely nominal or political in character. At times, her lack of interest in theology has been mistaken for a lack of interest in religion. Unlike her father and indeed her brother, she was no amateur theologian, and had little time for the polemical theologians of her own day. But she was a regular reader of scripture, especially the Psalms. Theologically lukewarm and politique as it may have been, her Protestantism was genuine enough. After all, an option for some sort of Protestantism was almost genetically programmed. As the daughter of Anne Boleyn she literally embodied Henry VIII's break with Rome. Illegitimate or not, she was the eldest child of the English Reformation, even if it was as much the political as the theological inheritance that shaped her destiny. Anne herself had more than flirted with evangelical doctrines in her brief reign, and was enrolled among the Protestant martyrs by John Foxe in his account of the sufferings of the English Church (his *Acts and Monuments*, or 'Book of Martyrs' as it came to be known, which he published with a dedication to Elizabeth in 1563).Yet Elizabeth could hardly have remembered her mother. It was the circumstances of her birth, rather than any sentimental attachment to her mother's memory, that determined her religious stance. As the papacy had never recognised Henry's divorce as valid, while the king claimed that his marriage to Catherine of Aragon was against scripture itself, it was on the authority of the Bible alone, of the Bible as opposed to the Catholic Church, that Elizabeth based her very right to the throne, and in a sense her very right to life.

Had Elizabeth retained any kind of feeling for the Catholicism to which she had conformed during Mary's reign, no doubt some deal could have been struck with the papacy to sort out the troubled question of her legitimacy.Yet she was of the first generation to grow up out of communion with the Church of Rome, and therefore lacked that sympathy with the 'old religion' (as it was coming to be known) which still characterised the majority of her subjects. With no strong religious motive to seek the sanction of the Holy Father, there were three overwhelming reasons not to do so. Firstly, there were problems in English common law regarding the rights of inheritance of those born out of wedlock, problems which could not necessarily be resolved by papal dispensation – not strictly relevant to the inheritance of the throne, but with potentially nasty implications for it. From the Catholic point of view, Elizabeth could never be more than a legitimised bastard. From a Protestant point of view, which based its understanding of the forbidden and permitted degrees of marriage on the text of Leviticus, her birth could be reckoned legitimate before God and therefore in no need of further clarification before man. Secondly, to owe her throne to the grace of the pope would be to recognise some sort of papal political supremacy. But from her earliest youth Elizabeth had heard the papacy's political claims dismissed as tyrannical usurpations. Henry VIII's father might have been content with a degree of dependence on papal grace, but this would never do for his daughter. Lastly, and worst of all, to be *deemed* legitimate would be to acknowledge her illegitimacy, to accept the social taint of 'base birth' which even the fullness of papal power could not purge from the proud hearts of Europe's nobility.

Elizabeth may have been no theologian, but she remained a devout Protestant, in a manner more characteristic of the first generation of

Protestantism than of the strictly defined creeds which were crystallising in the later sixteenth century. Her translation of the *Mirror for the Sinful Soul* embodied the key Protestant doctrine of justification by faith alone, but expressed it in a moderate and conciliatory way which was still tenable, just, within the confines of traditional Catholicism. Its original author, Marguerite of Navarre, lived under Francis I of France in a church which was still more traditional than Henry VIII's Church of England, in which the young Elizabeth was brought up. Elizabeth, of course, grew up with English Protestantism, and felt in Mary's reign that the religion Mary was restoring was largely alien to her. Yet she retained from her youth a taste for a more liturgical and less intellectual religious life which kept her away from the black-and-white certainties of professional theologians. The prayers which she composed for her private use show a sincere religious faith, and a genuine trust in what she had called shortly after her accession 'the excedyng goodnes of God', which she believed had protected her through the 'difficult tymes' until her 'commyng to this our crowne'.

Whatever her religious views, they were not as strongly held as those of the Protestant exiles of Mary's reign, nor indeed as strongly held as those of Mary. Although Elizabeth had dragged her feet at first, she had conformed to the Mass under Mary, even if her later show of enthusiasm had not fooled many people. Mary had never conformed to the Book of Common Prayer under Edward. Though no coward, Elizabeth, unlike Mary, was not the stuff of which martyrs are made. This may have had something to do with their education. Mary's tutor, the Catholic Richard Fetherstone, had fled to Wales in 1534 in the hope of avoiding the oath to the first Act of Succession. Captured and thrown into the Tower, he was eventually attainted without trial and executed in 1540 for refusing to recognise Henry VIII as Supreme Head of the Church of England. Elizabeth's tutor, the Protestant Roger Ascham, conformed quietly under Mary, and was delighted to find himself appointed as her Latin Secretary. That said, Elizabeth indulged in relatively risk-free gestures which hinted at her real sympathies. When she finally bowed to the inevitable, and attended Mass, she complained throughout proceedings of a stomach-ache! The fine rosary which Mary gave her was never used or even worn: in Edward's reign, the rosary had become the badge of Mary's political affinity. In Elizabeth's reign, the rosary was once more banned. Later, Elizabeth clearly preferred the company of dutiful conformists such as herself – Cecil, Parker and Leicester – to the stiff-necked and hard-faced men who returned from abroad to fill most of the influential posts in her church hierarchy, men like John Jewel (Bishop of Salisbury), Edmund Grindal (Bishop of London) and William Whittingham (Dean of Durham).

Although Elizabeth's Protestant sympathies were already ingrained, her conformity under Mary must qualify our understanding of her Protestantism. Zealous Protestants saw the Mass as an abomination of blasphemous idolatry. Devout Catholics saw it as the making present of the sacred body and blood of Jesus Christ. Elizabeth saw it neither as the former nor as the latter: or she would either have refused to attend it in Mary's reign, or insisted on retaining it in her own. But this was just part and parcel of her general lack of interest in theology – which should not be confused with a lack of interest in religion. For Elizabeth, the liturgy of the Eucharist, whether as Catholic Mass or Protestant Communion, was still the ritual commemoration of the Last Supper, and for that reason a given of the Christian life. She preferred this ritual to be conducted in the vernacular, but even that waited upon the law of the land. Hence her own incomprehension at those Catholic Recusants who refused on theological grounds to attend the service of her

Church, which to her was nothing more than an English version of the Latin service. She did not deny them their doctrine of transubstantiation, and no one was to be executed in her reign for Eucharistic heresy, though Catholic priests, and even some lay people, were executed for celebrating or attending Mass – now defined by statute as treasonable offences.

The theological flimsiness of Elizabeth's Protestantism is equally evident in her complete insensitivity to the Puritan myth of 'the Word'. When Edmund Grindal, her second Archbishop of Canterbury (1575–83), urged upon her the importance of providing for the church an adequate supply of learned preachers, she replied that the Book of Homilies (a volume of off-the-peg sermons for the less able clergy) was more than enough preaching for anyone. Not only was the doctrine of the Homilies, although Protestant, less then wholly satisfactory in Puritan eyes, but there was a more disturbing failure on her part to appreciate the importance of the preached word, the word preached from the heart, at the core of Protestant spirituality. She herself frequently remarked that she would rather address God in prayer than hear him discussed in sermons. Not that she was averse to a good sermon. Thanks to her humanist education, she had an ear for rhetoric, as well as a knack for the well-turned phrase. But her taste in preachers was revealing. She preferred the grandiloquence of Lancelot Andrewes, more obviously scholarly and rhetorical, to the plain style affected for the most part by more thoroughgoing Protestants. The preaching of Andrewes was closer to the baroque of the Jesuits (whose pulpit oratory enthralled the notoriously irreligious King Henry IV of France) than to the austere and affected simplicity of the Puritans. The sermon, even among devotees such as the Puritans, always had something of the stage about it. One suspects that it was amusement and intellectual pleasure, rather than spiritual enlightenment and edification, that Elizabeth most looked for from a preacher.

In many ways, however, Elizabeth's religion remains an enigma. She said that she would not open windows into men's souls. She certainly never opened any into her own. She was in religion, as in so much else, decisively ambiguous. All we can conclude from her ambiguity is that her religious life was not dominated by some consuming sense of Gospel truth or divine love. Systematic ambiguity may be attractive to the postmodern mind, but was hardly compatible with the profound faith of a Luther, a Calvin, or a Teresa of Avila. It goes without saying that Elizabeth left nothing remotely resembling the spiritual diary so characteristic of the Puritan. Nor did she leave much else. Her contempt for the fine points of theology to which so many of her contemporaries devoted their lives is summed up in her comment to a visiting French ambassador: 'there was only one Jesus Christ and one faith, and all the rest that they disputed about but trifles'. Historians have endeavoured to affiliate her with this or that creed, deducing systematic religious principles from stray comments and anecdotes that have come down to us. Her dismissal of candles during her coronation was a gesture redolent of the Protestant critique of Catholicism as idolatry and a religion of empty ceremonies. Yet she retained a cross and candles on the altar of the Chapel Royal, to the intense annoyance of her chaplains and bishops, who argued with her long, hard and often over these 'dregs of popery', which they rightly saw as dangerous (from their point of view) not only in themselves but also in the hope which they instilled into the hearts of the disaffected. The woman who walked out of a Mass at the elevation of the blessed sacrament (thus advertising her essential solidarity with the Protestants who had been burned in Mary's reign after showing similar disrespect to the sacrament) nevertheless had the wording of the Book of Common

Prayer amended in order to make it easier for the Catholics who had burned them to swallow the new communion (the amended wording was compatible with a Catholic understanding of the real presence of Christ in the sacrament).

What all the gestures really tell us, though, is that they are precisely that – gestures. They are not unconscious manifestations of Elizabeth's innermost thoughts and preferences, but carefully choreographed moves and shrewdly scripted sound bites designed to elicit particular responses from particular audiences at particular times. There was probably no better example on the stage of Tudor politics of someone who, as Thomas More had put it in his *Utopia*, knew how to improvise a part for herself in the drama unfolding around her. Elizabeth always played the appropriate part. Here and there we can cling on to something a little more solid. Her defence of church music is too lasting to be dismissed as a mere gesture. And her patronage of church musicians such as Thomas Tallis and William Byrd, who were notorious (if docile) Roman Catholics, shows that music could take precedence for her over both dogma and the requirements of obedience. Her musical taste was not without theological significance: the extremes of Protestantism represented by the

Puritans and by the Reformation in Switzerland looked with hatred upon the ornate musical styles of the Renaissance as an idolatry of the ear, a distraction from the worship of God in spirit and truth, every bit as damnable as the images and stained glass which had once decorated the interiors of churches. Yet we look in vain to Elizabeth for a textbook rationale of church music. What we hear in the Anglican musical tradition, which she did more than any other single person to found, is a testimony to her taste rather than to her theology.

The alteration of religion, then, was the first business to be transacted in Elizabeth's first parliament in 1559. One of the first surviving policy papers of the reign, entitled the 'Device for the Alteration of Religion', sets out the context of the problem and the plan for change with such brilliant clarity that it can only represent the thinking of William Cecil himself. Shrewdly assessing the dangers both at home and abroad, the 'Device' proposes swift but judicious change –

> At the next Parliament: so that the dangers be foreseen, and remedies therefore provided. For the sooner that religion is restored, God is the more glorified, and as we trust will be more merciful unto us,

and better save and defend Her Highness from all dangers.

Its plan seems, broadly, to have been followed. Even the 'Device', however, failed to anticipate the degree of opposition which the religious legislation would face. Although the exiguous record of parliamentary proceedings is difficult to interpret, what is beyond doubt is that the process was more contentious than any previous Tudor change of religion. Almost uniquely in the history of Tudor parliaments, there was concerted and sustained opposition to government proposals. Several bills were either flatly voted down or else subjected to wrecking amendments by the House of Lords (the House of Commons was usually even more subservient than the Lords to the legislative proposals of the Crown). The content of these bills is largely a matter for conjecture. No drafts survive, and the one-line descriptions in the sketchy parliamentary journals do not provide a reliable basis for analysis. But they were unwelcome to the House of Lords, whose temporal peers were split almost evenly in religion, and whose spiritual peers, the bishops (all of them selected or at least re-appointed by Mary Tudor), were determined to fight every inch of the way.

The bishops had a second forum for dissent, which they exploited to the full. Convocation, the representative body of the clergy, always sat at the same time as parliament, and was manned by the bishops (the upper house) and representatives of every diocese (the lower house), who were for the most part drawn from the ranks of the deans, archdeacons and canons who administered the church on the ground. In short, Convocation *was* the hierarchy of the Church of England. Led by Edmund Bonner, the Bishop of London (Cardinal Pole had died on the same day as Mary Tudor, and the see of Canterbury was therefore vacant), Convocation drew up and promulgated towards the end of February an uncompromising summary of Roman Catholic doctrine as the teaching of the Church of England. Never before had Convocation openly repudiated the religious policy of the Crown, and the government was clearly disturbed at the prospect of trying to pass religious legislation in the teeth of opposition from the entire hierarchy. Parliament was adjourned while the queen and her advisers worked out what to do next.

What was arranged was one of the familiar expedients of reforming governments in the sixteenth century, a public disputation on the relative merits of the old and the new religions, held in Westminster Abbey on 31 March. As the Crown held the ring, the reformers were able to define the terms and the topics of discussion. Rather than engage their opponents on such central issues as papal primacy, the sacrifice of the Mass, or the real presence, they chose instead to argue over the use of Latin in the liturgy, the administration of the chalice to the laity in communion, and the so-called 'private Mass'. In short, they shrewdly chose issues where they felt a better chance of victory, issues where the Catholic position depended crucially on the authority of the pope and medieval tradition rather than on the intrinsic merits of the theological case. The Catholic party at the disputation was on the back foot from the start, and in fact the combat was never properly joined, as the two sides bickered fruitlessly over procedural technicalities – a situation which, as the Catholics were the ones complaining, made them look as though they lacked the stomach for a fight. Two of the Catholic bishops were arbitrarily imprisoned for their role in this debacle, and the Catholic party as a whole was to a certain extent discredited, especially in London.

Catholic resistance in the House of Lords was in consequence weakened. The spiritual peers were depleted in numbers, and the Catholics among the temporal peers were somewhat demoralised. When religious legislation came back to the Lords after the Easter break, it was in the form of two separate acts, one re-establishing the royal supremacy, the other re-enacting the Book of Common Prayer. The Act of Supremacy went through with the support of the temporal peers, only one of whom joined the ten bishops present in opposing it. The Act of Uniformity, however, was opposed by nine temporal peers as well as nine bishops, and passed by only three votes – with two bishops in custody, and with Goldwell (Bishop-elect of Oxford) and Feckenham (Abbot of Westminster) prevented from attending. This is not to suggest that there was any real risk of Elizabeth's Reformation being frustrated. Even if the bishops had been all present, all Elizabeth needed to do was to create a few new temporal peers. It was simply easier to stop a few spiritual peers voting.

One of the few unambiguous features of Elizabeth's religious position is her utter commitment to maintaining the settlement of the Church, which was the first business of her first parliament. The phrase 'Elizabethan Settlement' which in the twentieth century became attached to the achievement of 1559 could in many ways hardly be less appropriate. It is unlikely that anybody apart from the queen herself envisaged what was done as a 'settlement' with all the finality implied by that term. There had been too many sharp turns in religious policy in too few years for anyone to feel confident about stability. And if few expected it, still fewer hoped for it. Catholics hoped for another turn of fortune's wheel (as we can see from those countless parishes which held onto their Catholic liturgical gear for years after its use was made illegal), while Protestants hoped for further reformation to complete the construction of the new Jerusalem (as we can see from those revealing letters which leading Protestants sent to their coreligionists in Switzerland). 'Semper eadem', however, was Elizabeth's motto: nowhere more so than in her religious position after 1559. Time and again pressure for change bubbled up. First it came from her own bench of bishops, although their impotence even to remove that cross and those candles from her chapel gave them a healthy respect for her will, so that they encouraged their subordinates to raise the cry for reform. Subsequently it came from the lower clergy and even from enthusiastic laymen agitating in parliament. Invariably it was resisted.

When many parish ministers threw off their vestments in the mid-1560s, demanding the right to celebrate the liturgy in little more than plain clothes, it was Elizabeth who compelled her Archbishop of Canterbury to impose uniformity and uniform upon them. Here she showed a characteristic blend of rigidity and cunning. Everyone agreed that vestments were 'things indifferent' (often described by the Greek word 'adiaphora'). But while the zealous Protestants, soon to be known as Puritans, argued that therefore the authorities should not make such an issue out of wearing them, the authorities in their turn argued that the dissidents should not make such an issue out of refusing them. But it was Elizabeth who chose to make vestments a test of obedience, and thus to invest an intrinsically marginal issue with great extrinsic significance. Yet her inflexible policy was shrewdly implemented. She held back from investing her personal authority and charisma in the matter, and compelled the unfortunate Matthew Parker, her Archbishop of Canterbury, to promulgate orders on the subject over his own name, thus diverting on to him the brunt of the reformers' ire.

Nor was there ever any prospect of Elizabeth yielding to Puritan pressure for abolishing bishops and introducing 'Presbyterian' church government. Elizabeth's essential social conservatism would always have prejudiced her against such a policy, and probably her education confirmed that temperamental inclination. Roger Ascham tells us that her theological reading in her schoolroom days included the writings of Cyprian of

Carthage, a bishop of the early church whose letters and treatises firmly upheld the doctrine of what is sometimes called 'monarchical episcopacy'. No reader of Cyprian in her formative years was likely to feel much sympathy for the alternative model of collegiate church government worked out by Calvin and his followers: a model in which local churches were presided over by godly oligarchies which elected their pastor and controlled access to the sacrament of communion. She was always going to prefer the clear vertical lines of authority which characterised the traditional ecclesiastical hierarchy to the more horizontal patterns of power which typified Calvinist church organisation, and were often associated with republican governments.

Agitation for Presbyterianism first appeared around 1570, and periodically resurfaced thereafter in the 1570s and 1580s, in speeches in parliament, in pamphlet broadsides, and in local initiatives to establish a semblance of Presbyterianism on a voluntary basis. Elizabeth's third, last and favourite Archbishop of Canterbury, John Whitgift (1583-1604, the only clergyman ever appointed to her Privy Council), actually first won her favour by means of his lengthy controversy with England's leading Presbyterian theoretician, Thomas Cartwright. Whitgift's reasonable observation that the Presbyterian model was rich in potential for faction and divisiveness was precisely how Elizabeth herself saw it. There was more to Puritanism than Presbyterianism, but the Presbyterian inclinations of many Puritans helped consolidate Elizabeth's prejudice against the movement as a whole. She ordered her bishops to stamp out any ecclesiastical initiatives which smacked to her of disobedience. Many of her bishops sympathised at least with some elements in the Puritan programme. In December 1576, barely a year after his appointment as Archbishop of Canterbury, Grindal refused to implement her direct instructions to suppress 'prophesyings' (in essence, Bible-reading groups). As a result of his obduracy he was suspended from the exercise of his duties and deprived of the revenues of his see, remaining archbishop in name alone until his death in 1583. In Whitgift, Elizabeth found her ideal replacement for Grindal, and for the next twenty years he ruthlessly clamped down on Puritan activists and readily took the flak for her. This made him the particular butt of the 'Marprelate Tracts', a popular series of wickedly satirical pamphlets against the bishops published by a small group of outspoken Puritans in the years 1588–89. These tracts were in fact too successful for their own good. Not only were those responsible hunted down, but their irreverence towards authority enabled the bishops to exploit the traditional association between religious dissent and sedition in such a way as to discredit Puritanism in the eyes of important sections of the political elite.

Among the reasons for Elizabeth's refusal to contemplate further religious change was her personal animus against the figure who was becoming the international godfather of Protestantism, John Calvin. For it was in Calvin's adopted home, Geneva, that John Knox, in the darkest moments of the Marian repression, had penned and published his notorious *First Blast of the Trumpet against the Monstrous Regiment of Women*, a pungent little treatise which generalised from the unsatisfactory policies of female rulers in England, Scotland and the Netherlands (Mary Tudor, Mary of Guise and Mary of Hungary, all of them Catholics, and all of them at that time vigorously repressing heresy) and from a selective corpus of biblical evidence to construct a powerful theoretical case against the exercise of political authority by women.

This untimely tract appeared shortly before Elizabeth succeeded to the throne, and Knox bore the brunt of her displeasure. When he sought to return to Scotland, Elizabeth would not let him so much as set foot in her dominions, compelling him to take the slower and riskier sea route. Calvin also learned his lesson. Shortly after Elizabeth's accession he sent her a copy of his commentary on the Book of Isaiah, with a letter of congratulation. But William Cecil wrote back explaining that there was no chance of Elizabeth accepting the gift because she blamed Calvin personally for the publication of Knox's little effort. In vain Calvin pleaded that it was not he but the city council which controlled censorship in Geneva. This little equivocation deceived nobody. The damage had been done. Many years later, Elizabeth told a French ambassador that, notwithstanding rumours that she had never read anything but Calvin, she had simply never read any Calvin. Just as the 'obvious' Lutheran destiny of the English Reformation in the 1530s had been closed off by Henry VIII's ineradicable hatred for Luther, so now the equally 'obvious' Calvinist destination of the Reformation was closed off by Elizabeth's hatred for Calvin and Knox.

VI

SCOTLAND AND THE
SUCCESSION:
1559–1568

Religious concerns dominated the politics of
Elizabeth's reign from start to finish. Elizabeth's
regime was as keen as those of Edward and
Henry before it to encourage the Reformation
cause in Scotland as a means of closing
England's backdoor to potential enemies. With
Mary Queen of Scots married to the Dauphin
Francis, the prospect that the French might
invade through Scotland was a very real one,
raised in the 'Device for Alteration of Religion'
as one of the potential obstacles to be faced in

returning the Church of England to the Protestant fold. When, a few months after the alteration of religion in England, Henry II's death in a jousting accident placed the young Dauphin on the French throne as Francis II, the Scottish problem assumed menacing proportions. Francis was politically in the pocket of his wife's powerful uncles, the militantly Catholic Duke of Guise and his like-minded brothers. It was Guise who had retaken Calais, and now that the English were heretics as well as enemies, he would be doubly keen to renew hostilities against them. The response to the Scottish threat was essentially that adumbrated in the 'Device', namely 'to help forward their divisions, and especially to augment the hope of them who incline to good religion'.

In the meantime, and despite Elizabeth's obstructive attitude, John Knox had returned to Scotland in May 1559, and had fomented widespread religious unrest. In this troubled context, the Protestant 'Lords of the Congregation', a band of lords united by a formal bond to promote their religious cause through political action, moved to overthrow the French Regent of Scotland, Mary of Guise, in October. However, Scottish politics remained typically tumultuous, and the case for English intervention, which Cecil put forward in a policy paper of August

1559, was strong. Cecil argued that swift financial and military assistance to the rebel lords would be decisive in securing religious change in Scotland and breaking the French connection. In the religiously divided context of European politics, England and Scotland would be drawn together by their shared Protestant commitments, and their time-honoured enmity would be turned into lasting friendship.

Queen Elizabeth, however, was not so easily convinced, and the Scottish crisis of 1559-60 was the first of many episodes in which we can the tortuous emergence of policy from the complex relationship between Elizabeth and her trusted chief minister and other advisers. Where Cecil's approach was a curious blend of religious principle and *realpolitik*, notable earlier in the reign for a real breadth of strategic vision, Elizabeth's was compounded of caution, parsimony and an ideology which privileged the values of kingship over the values of the gospel to the extent that they might compete. On those occasions when her instincts and Cecil's did not immediately converge, the result was hesitation. Throughout her reign, hesitancy and parsimony were continually picked out by her councillors, in their private correspondence and comments, as her besetting political failings (though both traits may well have saved her from numerous expensive mistakes!). In this early case, the hesitation was compounded by the fact that Cecil, although clearly Elizabeth's chief minister, had not as yet established the dominant position on the Privy Council that he was to hold in later years. There were other, more cautious voices to whom the queen seemed inclined to listen, maintaining that the dire financial straits of the Crown ruled out intervention in Scotland. She herself now first displayed the reluctance she often showed later for interfering in the domestic affairs of other kingdoms. She had a high view of the duties of obedience which subjects owed to their princes. This had, after all, been the relentless message of English preaching throughout her childhood, and was at the core of the whole concept of the royal supremacy. So she was far from relishing the evident hypocrisy in encouraging the subjects of other monarchs to commit what she condemned as mortal sin in her own.

The resurgence of the Regent's party in Scotland, which retook Edinburgh in November, brought matters to a head. Cecil had already extracted some grudging financial aid for the lords. Now direct military assistance was called for. But Elizabeth remained so set against it that Cecil asked to be relieved of the burdens of office. Only this threat, it seems, changed her mind. First her navy and then, in March 1560, an army of a few thousand men went into action on behalf of the Protestant faction in Scotland. The forces engaged were hardly adequate to the task, but fortune smiled on Elizabeth and the English. Religious tensions in France prevented effective aid from that quarter, making the English contribution decisive. William Cecil himself was sent north to Scotland to negotiate a peace, and his task was facilitated by the death of Mary of Guise on 11 June. The Treaty of Edinburgh, signed on 6 July, removed almost all French troops from Scotland and excluded Frenchmen from high Crown office. The Lords of the Congregation took over, and in August 1560 pushed a Protestant Reformation through parliament, repudiating the papacy, suppressing the monasteries, and prohibiting the Mass. There was no clear doctrinal statement – but then England itself had not yet seen the Thirty-Nine Articles. However, with John Knox dominant in the kirk, a fully Calvinist settlement was only a matter of time. The solution was not ideal from the point of view of England and of Elizabeth. There was no royal supremacy, and while bishops were not actually abolished, they were marginalised. Moreover, the death of Francis II in December 1560 made Mary Stuart's eventual return inevitable, which in turn posed a new threat to the stability of the settlement. Nevertheless, the Protestant regime in Scotland had nowhere to turn for support other than to England.

The triumph in Scotland sealed Cecil's place at the heart of Elizabeth's government. Although Elizabeth, as a monarch and a woman, continued to see the world from a very different perspective from his, she would never treat his advice with disdain, and for the rest of his long life (he died in 1598) no one challenged his primacy in policy advice.

The complex interplay of religion and politics was just as evident in the second foreign policy venture of Elizabeth's reign, an attempt to exploit growing religious conflict in France in order to regain Calais. In 1562 the Protestant party in France, known as the Huguenots, sought English financial support in the civil war which everyone could see was coming. By the Treaty of Hampton Court (August 1562), England agreed to provide men and money in return for the cession of Dieppe and Le Havre (then known in English as Newhaven) until such time as Calais was handed back. Elizabeth was more enthusiastic for this venture than she had been for the Scottish expedition. Again, this was a matter of the royal perspective. Elizabeth shared to the full her sister's sense of national disgrace at the loss of Calais, calling it 'a matter of continual grief to this realm'. She was therefore understandably attracted by the dream that she might 'have this our Calais returned to us', not just for honour but for the sake of enhancing still more the contrast between herself and the late Mary Tudor. Cecil, on the other hand, was less keen, already on record as judging Calais a drain on the exchequer and its loss a blessing in disguise. Support for Elizabeth came from her favourite, Robert Dudley, whose brother Ambrose, Earl of Warwick, was put in command of the troops which occupied Le Havre and Dieppe in October 1562.

This time, events vindicated Cecil's scepticism. Whereas in Scotland the English intervention could be presented as an aid in the struggle for liberation, in France it was manifestly predatory, notwithstanding the religious dimension. Once a peace was brokered between Catholics and Huguenots, both sides turned against the old enemy. Le Havre surrendered in summer 1563, showing how difficult it would have been to hold Calais against the might of France. Indeed, the loss of Calais under Mary was probably another stroke of luck for Elizabeth, for it would surely have fallen before too long in any case, and Elizabeth was therefore spared the personal humiliation of losing it. If the Le Havre adventure consolidated Cecil's position by bearing further witness to his sound judgement, it also confirmed Elizabeth's fundamentally non-militarist prejudices. Not for another twenty years would royal troops cross the Channel. During that time, the only military actions that Elizabeth sanctioned were against her own rebellious subjects, once in England, repeatedly in Ireland.

The love of gesture and the concern for image which emerge from an analysis of Elizabeth's apparently 'revealing' actions and sayings on the subject of religion offer us the key to her political character. For these same traits were almost always evident in her actions and sayings, whatever the subject. While we can learn something from this, we must be properly humble and realise that we can learn very little more than Elizabeth wished us to learn – and that often these lessons are rather suspect. The queen could be hard to read. Late in her reign an ambassador commented on how, during their conversation, she would often digress from the subject in hand. But he was unsure whether this was done deliberately, in order to gain time, or was simply an unself-conscious part of her character. Life at Elizabeth's Court was carefully stage-managed. The formal manner in which she sometimes greeted foreign ambassadors and visitors was designed to impress them with her wealth, power and security. The splendidly decorated Presence Chamber in her palace, with its throne beneath a cloth of estate to denote her royal rank, the well-built young gentlemen guarding the door, the handful of elegant noblemen and ladies-in-waiting or maids-of-honour disporting themselves gracefully around it, and one or two grave councillors on hand to ensure that the proceedings were properly recorded – and of course at the centre of it all, the person of the queen herself, striking and attractive in her youth, bewigged and heavily made-up in her later years, but always gorgeously attired in dresses remarkable for the richness of their cloth, the complexity of their design, the finesse of their workmanship, and the brilliance of the jewels which adorned them – all this carefully co-ordinated display invariably sent the right message to the bedazzled visitor.

There were less formal exercises as well. One ambassador commented on how Elizabeth made her entrance on one occasion in an especially dignified manner, expressly so 'that I might see her while she pretended not to see me'. Special scenes might be staged for the benefit of ambassadors and their foreign masters. Thus, early in the reign, Elizabeth's oldest companion, Katherine Ashley, threw herself on her knees before the queen in the presence chamber, upbraiding her for her familiarity with Dudley and urging her to make an honest woman of herself by marriage. Notwithstanding Ashley's years of intimacy with Elizabeth, it is hard to see her making quite so bold without some strong steer from above. For the scene gave Elizabeth the pretext to explain herself and to defend her good name and her favour for Dudley. Many years later, when the negotiations for a possible marriage between Elizabeth and the Duke of Anjou were underway, Leicester himself took the starring role in a remarkably similar scene. He appeared before the queen and, with otherwise incredible audacity, demanded whether or not she was still a virgin. It can hardly be thought that, with Elizabeth at the height of her powers, he would have dared question (or even challenge) her in such an intimate matter without her express instructions. But the point was of course to set French minds at rest about the relationship between the queen and her favourite early in the reign. Had Leicester himself slept with her, he would not have needed to ask!

We can detect the hand of the director behind these scenes by comparing them with those plainly unscripted scenes in which unwelcome gestures were made by her subjects, and she in turn was invited to respond with gestures that were far from her purposes. When Sir Richard Shelley, a young Catholic gentleman, dared to cast at the feet of the queen as she walked in her Whitehall gardens a petition seeking a limited toleration for her Catholic subjects, she did not seize upon the opportunity to dispense mercy as St Louis of France had once dispensed justice, beneath the oak tree, to those who brought him their griefs and grievances. Shelley was put under arrest, thrown into gaol, and left until he died.

Elizabeth's sense of theatre, though, could also result in performances which verged on the comic. The French ambassador André Hurault, sent on a mission to her Court in 1957, related her curious habit of tugging the front of her dress open down to the navel so to expose her midriff with its white and delicate skin, which at that stage of her life she presumably imagined showed to better effect than the wrinkled skin of her bosom. Despite this, and the coquettishness of her having greeted him in her nightgown when he was granted his first audience, and of her speaking of her beauty whenever she could, he remained favourably impressed, commenting on the dignity of her manners and deportment and on the vigour of her mind and body.

Parliament was another target of the queen's carefully planned displays of personality. She inherited her father's ability to win round that occasionally wilful and noisy institution. But where he had overawed with his physical presence, Elizabeth employed the power of words, skilfully varying her tone between gentleness and wrath. Although entire history books have been written to document the rise of 'opposition' to Elizabeth in parliament, in fact Elizabeth managed her parliaments effectively enough. The only serious opposition she ever faced there was over religion, in 1559, and that was soon overcome – and her largely episcopal opponents were soon relieved of their seats in the House of Lords. Far from parliament opposing Elizabeth, it was more often she that opposed parliament. In the course of her reign, many bills failed to become statutes because she took against them and denied them the royal assent. And while this was sometimes because they were politically offensive to her (as with certain proposals for harsher treatment of Catholics), it also seems that at times she did it simply to show who was in charge. Upon other occasions, Elizabeth found herself in receipt of unwanted advice, especially from her loyal House of Commons. The underlying problem here was her status as a woman. It was impossible for a chamber full of politically aware and opinionated gentlemen not to feel that, on a whole range of issues, from religion to economic regulation, they knew better than she did, and it was equally hard for them to deny her the benefit of their superior wisdom.

The occasional imprisonment of recalcitrant MPs, however, combined with the judicious treatment (now conciliatory, now contemptuous) of delegations from the Commons enabled her to maintain an adequate working relationship with parliament. The Lords, her 'cousins' by contemporary etiquette, were never a cause for concern once she had got rid of the Catholic bishops in 1559. At times Elizabeth was excessively anxious about the tendency of the Commons to infringe her 'prerogative' by debating matters of high policy without her authorisation. But the high view of kingship which underlay this anxiety was by no means an inexplicable foible. It was simply her memory of the kingship of her father. Like Mary, she knew that she could never have quite the hold over the subjects that he had attained. But she did rather more than Mary to emulate him as far as she could. She was always proud of her physical resemblance to him, evident in her bearing and her red hair. And she frequently invoked his memory, his example and his legacy in her public comments – most famously in her speech to the troops at Tilbury during the Armada campaign, where the 'heart and stomach of a king' which she claimed were hidden in her own 'weak body of a woman' were most certainly the heart and stomach of Henry VIII.

Elizabeth certainly used her femininity to great effect in the political arena. Of course, it did not exactly compensate for the defect of her birth – not her illegitimacy but her sex. Her repeated comments about her father, and her evident pride in being his daughter, show that she was a woman who lived always with the consciousness of not being a man. Indeed, her remark to a French ambassador in 1562, made in justifying her policy towards France, that she was 'the true and most obedient daughter of the late King Henry, King of England, her lord and father', hints at all these sensitivities. But she made the best of it. Courtly love was the language of her court. She expected as a matter of course to hear from the lips of her male favourites and servants effusions fit for Renaissance sonnet-eers or nineteenth-century romantic novelists. Throughout her life she fished shamelessly for compliments when conversing with men. The string of handsome and charming youths who shook a nice leg at a dance would not have disgraced a Hollywood starlet. When men such as Leicester found themselves out of favour, they earned their recovery by amorous letters or small-talk which became ever more extravagant as the ageing queen's charms faded. The conventions of courtly love, in which the social precedence of men over women was inverted by the image of the woman as the dominant, even tyrannical, partner in relationships, and that of the man as the strong made weak and dependent by passion, furnished a handy metaphor for the political inversion in which those involved found themselves, and helped make the unprecedented situation a trifle less unfamiliar.

The two chief priorities of domestic politics when Elizabeth came to the throne were religion and the succession. But while the first problem was solved almost at once, the second was never solved at all. Indeed, it was never seriously addressed by the queen herself, although it constantly preoccupied her ministers and many of her subjects. In one sense, the solution was obvious. Elizabeth would marry a suitable prince or nobleman and would bear him children, preferably boys.

This, however, was where the problem became complicated. For Elizabeth showed little if any intention of proceeding towards the consummation for which so many of her subjects so devoutly wished. From the earliest days of her reign, her reported views on marriage ranged from mere aversion to undisguised contempt.

In 1561, Archbishop Parker told William Cecil that, in a discussion of the marriage of the clergy, Elizabeth had spoken with such 'bitterness of the holy estate of matrimony that I was in a horror to hear her'. While some of these remarks can be discounted as characteristic role-playing, and others as characteristic conversational shock tactics, they are reported with such frequency and consistency that we should certainly take them seriously. Coupled with her often expressed preference for virginity and the single life, they give the impression of a woman who was simply not prepared to resolve the problem of the succession in the orthodox fashion.

However, there has long been debate over Elizabeth's intentions with regard to marriage, as over much else concerning her, precisely because she herself was prone to be obscure and ambiguous about her intentions. Even at the start of her reign, when foreign princes jostled for the privilege of marriage to Europe's most eligible spinster, there were contradictory rumours circulating around the queen's court. The rumour that Elizabeth had some physical incapacity for marriage is frequently reported from the earliest days, as are comments from Elizabeth's own lips in favour of virginity and against marriage in general and childbirth in particular. Dr Huick, her personal physician, who had known her many years, reckoned in the 1560s that she was physically incapable of sexual relations. On the other hand, at much the same time a committee of physicians judged her fit to bear children. Many years later, when she was forty-five and in the midst of negotiations for a marriage with the Duke of Anjou, another committee of physicians and ladies-in-waiting convinced Cecil that there was no reason why Elizabeth should not, even at this improbable age, bear a child. But despite their privileged knowledge of Elizabeth's bodily functions, the sceptical historian might observe that, if the truth really was otherwise, neither of these committees had much reason to report it. Elizabeth was notoriously sensitive to what she chose to see as aspersions upon her beauty and charm – the Earl of Leicester's secret marriage to Lettice Knollys was interpreted as one such affront – and might not have reacted too well to aspersions upon her essential femininity, notwithstanding her own explicit contempt for marriage and childbirth.

If there was not in fact a physical incapacity for marriage, it has been suggested that perhaps she had some sort of psychological hang-up about it, although opinions differ as to whether this went back to her experiences in the household of Sir Thomas Seymour or was simply a result of jealousy and frustration or indeed of sexual orientation. What is clear is that Elizabeth reacted extremely badly to marriage or even contemplation of marriage on the part of men who were close to her. Sometimes this can be put down to political rather than personal considerations. Members of the royal family were not allowed to marry without the consent (in effect, without the arrangement) of the sovereign. Thus when in the 1560s Lady Catherine Grey married Edward Seymour, Elizabeth's reaction – to throw them both in gaol – was no different from that of her father to the marriage of Lord Thomas Howard and Lady Margaret Douglas in the 1530s. The Duke of Norfolk's plan to marry Mary Queen of Scots comes into the same category. Even though Mary was not Elizabeth's subject, it was clearly incumbent upon the duke to inform his queen of his intentions, and the expectation of refusal which understandably deterred him from broaching the issue need not have rested upon any perception of the queen's emotional hostility to marriage.

Nevertheless, Elizabeth's peculiar reactions to marriage extended beyond the blood royal to almost any marriage contracted by men or women of her Court. Her favourites almost invariably concealed their marriages from her as long as possible, a subterfuge which inevitably exacerbated her wrath when the marriages inevitably came to light. After the row following Leicester's second marriage, to Lettice Knollys in the later 1570s, he was in due course forgiven and restored to favour. But his wife was never again allowed to come to Court. Elizabeth took umbrage when Sir Philip Sidney married the daughter of Sir Francis Walsingham in 1583, much to the annoyance of the latter, who complained that he was hardly of such exalted rank that the queen should interest herself in his family affairs. Similar stories of royal rage at the marriages of courtiers or maids-of-honour could be almost endlessly duplicated. One victim remained in disgrace so long that he died in prison. Elizabeth's bishops and clergy also suffered from her attitude to marriage. She refused to allow the wives of bishops to accompany their husbands to Court, and as long as she was on the throne, the law permitting the marriage of priests, which had been repealed by Mary, was not restored to the statute book.

Doubts or speculations about the queen's sexual orientation, however, may be easily laid to rest. Whatever her attitudes to marriage and sexual intercourse, she manifestly enjoyed the company of men. Her relationship with Robert Dudley in the early years of her reign appeared to Court and Council alike as nothing less than courtship. The complex rituals of flirtation and courtly love with which she often surrounded her dealings with men at Court and on the Council likewise reflected conventional assumptions about relations between the sexes, besides providing a convenient grammar and vocabulary with which to negotiate the existential discomfort for noble adult males of finding themselves in the unaccustomed position of dependence upon and service to a woman. Their situation could be rendered more palatable by being decked out as that of lovers seeking the favour of some damsel out of a chivalric romance. Hence the renewed vogue for chivalric and Arthurian literature which arose in Elizabethan times (and soon fell out of fashion thereafter, remaining in obscurity until rescued in the age of romanticism and the neo-gothic), seen at its most elaborate in the complex allegories of Spenser's unfinished Protestant epic, *The Faerie Queene.*

If, in her relationships with her more handsome courtiers, Elizabeth indulged in that language of formal flirtation which scholars call 'courtly love', she has nevertheless gone down in history as the 'Virgin Queen'. Vulgar rumour and the more malicious tongues of her Catholic enemies were quick to impugn her virginity, especially in the early years when her intimacy with Robert Dudley was an open secret. As late as 1581 one Henry Hawkins was saying that Elizabeth had had five children by Dudley, and only went on progress in order to give birth in secret. Yet there has never been any serious reason to question her boast. However far she might have gone with Dudley, she cannot have gone that far. For Elizabeth to have lost her virginity before marriage would have been an intolerable political risk. Kings and princes might sow their wild oats: royal bastards were nothing more than testimony to royal virility. But the sexual double standard was firmly in place in Tudor England, and for a queen to bear an illegitimate child would have been political suicide, earning her the fatal contempt of her own nobility. Catholic propagandists would have had a field day. Mary Queen of Scots provided Elizabeth with an object lesson here, for her tangled matrimonial and sexual career did nothing to cement the loyalty of a traditional aristocracy. Elizabeth's relationship with Dudley aroused enough resentment as it was. There is no telling what the Duke of Norfolk, or even the impeccably loyal Earl of Sussex, might have done if Elizabeth had borne Dudley's love-child. Henry's bastard might occupy the throne: but not Dudley's whore.

As the degree of interest both at Court and at large shows, her relationship with Robert Dudley was widely expected to end in marriage, notwithstanding her own disdain for marriage and the fact that Dudley himself already had a wife. When his first wife, Amy Robsart, died suddenly in 1560, the possibility of the match became more real, although the fact that she had died in suspicious circumstances, by breaking her neck in a fall downstairs, put a new obstacle on the path. To the aristocratic jealousies focused on Dudley himself was added the risk of guilt by association. By 1562, the time had come to end the affair. In one of those stage-managed set-pieces, Elizabeth broke things off with Dudley in front of her nobles and courtiers in the Presence Chamber, telling him in a towering rage that she would never marry him or anyone of such low rank.

For all the peculiarities and inconsistencies of Elizabeth on the subject of her own marriage and on marriages contracted in her Court circle, it would be risky to attempt long-distance psychoanalysis in search of the explanation. Her objections to marriage are expressed in thoroughly rational terms, ranging from her own disinclination to the married state to her clear perception of the political problems attendant upon marrying a foreign prince. Mary

Tudor's marriage to Philip of Spain had been deeply unpopular, owing to the general fear of a subordination of the realm to foreign interests. After 1559, the religious situation complicated the problem of a foreign marriage still further. The only foreign princes of a suitable status were Catholics, which was unacceptable to most of her closest advisers. And even those of the second rank were Lutherans, which was not much better, especially in the eyes of her bishops.

Finally, there was Elizabeth's personal experience of marriage as a spectator. The Tudor age was not sentimental about marriage, and Elizabeth was shrewd enough to draw reasonable conclusions from what she saw around her. Her own mother's marriage had ended on the block, and the rest of her father's matrimonial record would hardly have filled her with enthusiasm for the holy state. The one wife of Henry's with whom she had established a close relationship, Catherine Parr, had died in labour. Her elder sister's marriage was a palpable disaster. Nor was her cousin, Mary Queen of Scots, conspicuously well-served by the immature boy, the feckless youth, and the reckless adventurer with whom she successively linked herself. Leicester's first marriage, another failure, had ended in obscure tragedy. Elizabeth herself knew well enough the authority that contemporary opinion vested in husbands over their wives, and was probably reluctant to imperil her sovereign position by submitting herself to any man in any degree. Mary Tudor had looked on marriage as her destiny. Elizabeth certainly did not, and given her inclinations and her experience, her decision not to marry was in many ways a coolly sensible one.

Elizabeth's evident lack of haste towards marriage, however, unsettled those of her subjects who found themselves in power under the Protestant regime. The petition for her to marry put forward by her first parliament in 1559 was doubtless made more in expectation than hope. But Elizabeth's brush with mortality in 1562, when she almost died of smallpox, concentrated minds wonderfully. Doubts are evident in the anxiety of her second parliament in 1563, which saw some agitation for a statutory declaration of the succession, to exclude the Stuart line still more decisively by settling the inheritance upon the remaining Grey sisters and their descendants. Lady Catherine Grey, second of the three sisters, had borne two sons to Edward Seymour (notwithstanding the annulment of their marriage on Elizabeth's instructions), which made this line a particularly attractive option. Elizabeth fobbed off this petition with some typically ambiguous promises, but the parliament of 1566 returned to the issue still more persistently, with the evident encouragement of a number of members of the Privy Council. Elizabeth's reaction this time was volcanic. She summoned representatives of both Lords and Commons and informed them briskly that her marriage was a matter for her prerogative and no business of theirs. It took several further interventions to calm parliament down, but in the end Elizabeth emerged, having both made her point and avoided the issue, with the loyalty and gratitude of her subjects' representatives. She had not decided to marry, she had not promised to marry, and she had not made any other provision for the succession. Nor would she ever do so.

VII

MARY QUEEN OF SCOTS AND THE CATHOLIC PROBLEM: 1568–1580

The question of the succession was further complicated by Mary Queen of Scots, who had been a threat to the stability of the Elizabethan regime from the very start, when she quartered the arms of England with those of Scotland and France in what was an implicit claim if not to the throne then at least to the succession. For the rest of her tragic life, the English crown was the supreme object of her desire, and her aspirations were among the crucial influences on Elizabethan politics and on Elizabeth's personal life. Time and again, however, events conspired to frustrate Mary of legitimate hopes and less worthy ambitions. English victory in Scotland in 1560 ensured the success of the Reformation there, and fatally weakened the position of her Scottish allies and French relatives. Yet that was not too much of a problem as long as she was married to the King of France, for ultimately the might of France would have been thrown into the balance to avenge the English insult to French honour. But the death of her husband, the unmanly Francis II, was a more telling blow. Not only was her own power drastically reduced, but so was the influence of her Guise cousins in French politics. Suddenly, Scotland was all that was left to a woman who had dreamed of bequeathing no less than four kingdoms: England, France, Scotland and Ireland. With nothing to be gained from remaining in France, she returned in 1561 to what was almost a foreign country, herself more French than Scottish in tastes and manners. Here, her policy was simple: to angle for recognition of her claim to the English succession. For her at least, in Dr Johnson's famous words, there was no nobler prospect than the high road that leads to England.

What Mary most sought from Elizabeth was some explicit acknowledgement as heir presumptive. However, she was in fact excluded from the English succession under the terms of the 1544 Act of Succession, which was still in force. Not that this counted for much. The same exclusion obviously extended to her son, James, and it did not stop him from taking the English throne in 1603. There can be no doubt that, in purely hereditary and customary terms, her claim to the throne was the strongest: she was descended from Henry VIII's elder sister, Margaret. And had the matter ever come to a head, she might well have been able to vindicate her claim against the statutorily based but hereditarily inferior claims of the Greys, descended from Henry's younger sister Mary. If the history of the Tudors had shown anything, it had shown that the express wills of princes and parliaments were as nothing beside the force of arms and the consensus of the people about the rights of heirs. But Mary never showed herself a shrewd politician: unlike Elizabeth she wore her heart on her sleeve, and had little of her English cousin's talents for dissimulation, equivocation and obscurity. She had a certain difficulty also in distinguishing fantasy from reality. Thus she simply refused to believe that Henry VIII's will and the 1544 statute had specifically excluded her from the succession, and repeatedly demanded to be shown authenticated copies. Yet it was so, and some of Elizabeth's problems lay here.

Only an Act of Parliament could formally have guaranteed the succession of Mary, and the parliaments which convened under Elizabeth were unlikely to sanction the succession of a Catholic. Moreover, Elizabeth had her own reasons for leaving the question of her successor wrapped in indecent obscurity. She knew from her own experience under Mary Tudor how the person of the heir to the throne became a focus for plots and opposition. Suspicious to the very core of her Tudor being, she had no desire to whet the assassin's knife with hope.

Mary Stuart's few years in power were characterised by an ineptitude and miscalculation which not only failed to win her the throne of England but also lost her that of Scotland. Her policy was always inconstant and often impenetrable. Her unpredictable changes of attitude towards her nobility and her idiosyncratic position over religion alienated substantial sections of political opinion in Scotland. Perhaps the most remarkable thing is that, as late as 1568, she could still muster enough support to fight a civil war: a tribute not to her own talent, although she seems to have had a remarkable personal charisma which enabled her to win over the most improbable enemies, but to the endemic vendettas of Scottish noble politics, which ensured that whoever was in power would never lack for rivals. More characteristic was her failure to appreciate even this fundamental reality of Scottish politics, which led her to take refuge in England (of all places) after her defeat in that war. The shrewd option was simply to concede the demands of her foes and patiently rebuild her position, as she had done before. Instead, she staked – and lost – everything on a wild throw of the dice, fleeing to England in 1568 in the hope of securing political and military support from Elizabeth: from Elizabeth the parsimonious and peace-loving Protestant; from Elizabeth, the one person in the world who had everything to gain from Mary's exclusion from politics. Thus began nearly two decades of residence in England during which her status declined gradually from that of an honoured if slightly troublesome guest through house arrest to an irksome and unpleasant confinement (in the hands of a singularly obnoxious Puritan zealot) as public enemy number one, living on sufferance, and finally to her execution amidst public rejoicing.

The handling of Mary neatly illustrates the strengths and weaknesses of Elizabeth's character and policy. From the start Elizabeth respected her cousin as a fellow sovereign. To that very limited extent, then, there was something in Mary's dream of support. Elizabeth felt too exposed to look with equanimity on the dispossession of a neighbouring sovereign by a clique of ambitious noble malcontents. On the other hand, her instinct for political survival prevented her from granting the personal interview on which Mary pinned her hopes. Perhaps Elizabeth feared lest she fall victim to the renowned charm of the Scottish queen. She may have remembered how her own position had improved when, after her long rustication, she had been summoned back to Mary Tudor's Court in 1555. Perhaps she was worried that Mary Stuart's tarnished reputation in matters of sexual relations and political manoeuvres might reflect upon her own (which had, after all, suffered enough from her protracted but unconsummated affair with Robert Dudley). Mary was suspected of serial adultery and conspiracy to murder. Most probably, Elizabeth feared the political consequences of giving second place at her court (and no lower place could have been accorded to a visiting sovereign) to someone who certainly had a record for plotting and intrigue. So Mary was kept firmly and safely at arm's length.

On the other hand, Elizabeth resisted long and hard the clamouring crescendo for Mary's execution. This had begun in 1569, for Mary's arrival had provoked within a year a plot to liberate her and overthrow Elizabeth with her political and religious establishment. The reliably Protestant parliaments of Elizabeth called for Mary's execution with monotonous regularity – often at the instigation of the Privy Council. Perhaps Elizabeth's reluctance to bow to this pressure showed some appreciation of how closely Mary Stuart's present position resembled her own former position under Mary Tudor back in the 1550s, when Mary was being pressed by a group of her councillors to seal her political achievement with Elizabeth's blood. Yet perhaps also we can see, between the reluctance to allow Mary to come to Court and the refusal to adopt the Machiavellian solution to a very real political problem, Elizabeth's own political limitations. Between reason and honour Elizabeth was putting Mary into an intolerable situation, virtually driving her into precisely the sort of intrigues that Elizabeth most feared. Faced with the growing certainty of life imprisonment not only without trial but without even the shadow of justice (as a sovereign, Mary was not even subject to Elizabeth's jurisdiction), it was only to be expected that Mary would conspire to bring about the only event that could possibly lead to her release – Elizabeth's death. Finally, Elizabeth was perfectly well aware how it would look if she consigned Mary to the scaffold. The action would inevitably be presented as one of cruelty and tyranny and inhumanity – as of course it was.

Mary's arrival immediately destabilised the still shaky structure of Elizabethan politics. For that old-fashioned section of the English nobility which wished to settle the doubts over the succession, which resented the political hegemony of William Cecil, and which regretted the divisiveness of the religious situation, Mary Queen of Scots actually looked more like a solution than a problem. As Elizabeth's reluctance to marry was increasingly apparent, the notion of marrying off Mary to an English nobleman seemed to some people the best of all possible worlds. And England's premier nobleman, the Duke of Norfolk, was happily an eligible middle-aged widower at that precise moment. The match held out the prospect of the succession secured to an English heir (Mary had proved that she could have children), the Elizabethan Church of England guaranteed by the duke (a confirmed if moderate Protestant), and the Catholics reconciled to a Catholic queen (and presumably enjoying a fair degree of toleration). Mary and Norfolk had agreed the marriage by the end of 1568, and spent 1569 working on English aristocrats and foreign ambassadors to try and give their plan unstoppable momentum. But

Norfolk and his allies shied away from broaching their plan with Elizabeth, and eventually it was she who, when the rumours became impossible to ignore, broached the subject with him, extorting a confession from him and brusquely commanding him to abandon any idea of going through with the marriage. Elizabeth had no intention of sanctioning Mary Stuart's claim to the throne, still less of strengthening her political position by allowing her to marry the richest man in her kingdom. Besides which, everyone knew that this marriage would leave Cecil's political position untenable, and Elizabeth had no intention of dismissing her chief councillor.

Norfolk had invested too heavily in his hopes to put them aside at the mere word of the queen, and retired in dudgeon to consider his options – which included raising the standard of rebellion. In the end, his nerve failed him, but two of his allies, the Catholic Earls of Northumberland and Westmorland, decided to make their move without his support, calling out their retainers in the name of the old religion and marching southwards with the intention of taking control of the person of the Scottish queen. Their plot was doomed from the moment that Mary herself was whisked away to the safety of the Midlands. Their followers melted away as a royal army marched northwards to reinforce the Earl of Sussex, then President of the Council of the North, based at York. The rising of the northern earls was put down with greater cruelty than any other Tudor rebellion. In the wake of the Pilgrimage of Grace, Henry VIII had demanded the execution of a man in every village north of the Trent, but the then Duke of Norfolk had wisely mitigated his severity in practice. After this much less serious rebellion, Henry's policy seems to have been implemented by his daughter. Some 900 men were hanged in the north-east of England, although Elizabeth claimed 'we have always been of our own nature inclined to mercy'. Cruelty to the little people, however, was mixed with an astonishing indulgence towards the main culprit, the Duke of Norfolk. His grandfather would never have dared show the degree of disobedience to Henry VIII which he had shown to Henry's daughter. But equally, Elizabeth herself was far less ready than her father to destroy her greatest subject. For all her insistence that she was every inch as much a monarch as her father, Elizabeth could do nothing about the cultural disadvantage conferred on her by her sex, and the relationship between sovereign and nobility could never be the same under a woman as under a man.

Norfolk, however, pursued his own destruction with unwonted steadiness of purpose.

Released from custody in August 1570, he was soon deep in intrigue with Spanish and papal agents once more, still with a view to marrying Mary. Little more than a year later he was back in the Tower, and in January 1572 he was convicted of high treason. Even so, it was four months before Elizabeth could be persuaded to sign his death warrant. Elizabeth was nothing like as ready as her father to set the heads of her nobility rolling around Tower Hill.

The northern earls had rallied their troops under a Catholic banner – quite literally, for it was the banner of St Cuthbert, traditionally housed at the shrine in Durham Cathedral, the banner under which the men of the north were accustomed to march against the Scots. This reminded Elizabeth and Cecil of the political risks inherent in religious division. Their public line, though, was to maintain that religion was just a pretence to conceal the rebels' real objective, 'the subduing of this realm under the yoke of foreign princes'. The lesson was hammered home by the untimely decision of Pope Pius V to excommunicate and depose Elizabeth as a heretic and a tyrant. The papal bull announcing this sentence, *Regnans in Excelsis* (known, like all papal bulls, from its opening words), appeared in February 1570, just as the last embers of revolt were being stamped out. Henceforth it was possible to argue that no good Catholic could be a loyal subject of the queen. This specious line of argument was invoked over the next twenty years to justify ever stricter penal laws against Catholics, laws which often in effect defined aspects of Roman Catholic faith or worship as high treason. The process began almost immediately in the 1571 parliament, where calls for the execution of Mary Stuart and Norfolk were accompanied by frenzied proposals for dealing with 'papists' – who were increasingly seen as the 'enemy within'. Reconciling and being reconciled to the Roman Catholic Church were made treasonable offences, and the possession of Catholic devotional objects which had received papal blessing became liable to the penalties of 'praemunire' (forfeiture of goods and imprisonment at Her Majesty's pleasure). A bill to levy heavy fines on Catholics who refused to take communion in their parish church failed only because Elizabeth herself exercised the royal veto. One of the few religious bills to which Elizabeth did give assent in that parliament was an act requiring all clergy holding benefices in the Church of England to subscribe to the Thirty-Nine Articles (the summary of its doctrine which had been agreed by Convocation in 1563) – thus making it harder for closet Catholics to stay inside or infiltrate the ministry of her church.

Religious and political tension increased throughout the reign, but most rapidly from

1580, when a new initiative by the Catholic refugee community in Europe began to bear fruit: training priests abroad and sending them back as missionaries. The mission to England in 1580–81 of two Jesuits, Robert Parsons and Edmund Campion, revivified the Catholic community, struck fear into their dedicated Protestant opponents, and astounded the nation in general. Touring the land and evading their pursuers for months, they reconciled hundreds of Catholics before Campion was captured and Parsons fled the country. Campion, having been tortured, was tried and executed under the old treason law, along with some other priests. But the charges were not especially convincing, and now that the Catholics had some appealing martyrs to set against the Protestant martyrs made famous by John Foxe, they were quick to celebrate them in print. The guiding spirit of the Catholic refugees abroad, William Allen, published his *Brief History of the Glorious Martyrdom of Twelve Reverend Priests, Father Edmund Campion and his Companions* in 1582, and William Cecil thought it worth his while to write a reply, *The Execution of Justice in England* (1583).

Amidst the panic inspired by the mission of Campion and Parsons, new measures against Catholics were multiplied and, more to the point, were purposefully implemented. (The gulf between law and enforcement was even wider in the sixteenth century than it is in the twenty-first.) By the 1590s, thousands upon thousands of 'recusants' (as those who refused to attend Church of England services were known) were being regularly fined huge sums, while hundreds of Catholics, both priests and those who sheltered them, were being imprisoned, banished or even executed. About 120 Catholic priests were executed over the next twenty years, most of them under new laws which simply declared it treason to have been ordained as a Catholic priest abroad. But in an age when religion was the most important issue in the political arena, arguments about whether the executions were for political or religious reasons were essentially verbal. Those who lobbied in parliament for harsher measures were not bothered about such distinctions. Nor were Catholics unduly worried by this quibbling. English Catholic victims were given a prominent place in a pictorial martyrology published in 1587 by Richard Verstegan, the *Theatre of the Cruelties of the Heretics of Our Times*. These images did as much to shape the Catholic imagination as was done on the other side by the images of Protestants suffering under Mary Tudor, depicted in Foxe's 'Book of Martyrs'.

Elizabeth's claim that she did not seek to open windows into men's souls was looking

1 Drawing of Archbishop Warham by Hans Holbein. It is easy to believe
Catherine of Aragon's claim that this lugubrious clergyman's mantra was 'the
wrath of the prince is death'. Yet, cautious though he was, his reluctance to assist
in Henry VIII's divorce process was probably stiffened by the prophecies of the
Kentish visionary Elizabeth Barton. His death in August 1532 thus removed a
crucial obstacle from the king's path.

2 Thomas Cranmer by Gerlach Flicke. As it was Cranmer who annulled Henry's first marriage and authorised his second, he was an especially suitable choice to stand as Elizabeth's godfather at her christening on 10 September 1533.

3 Executions for treason at Tyburn (near where Marble Arch stands today). The victims are dragged on hurdles to the gallows, hanged, and then disembowelled and cut into pieces which, after being boiled to preserve them better, were displayed on poles at the gates of the city. On Monday 20 April 1534, Elizabeth Barton and five priests who had supported her public opposition to Henry's divorce became Henry's first victims.

4 Henry VIII by Hans Holbein. Henry's memory loomed large in Elizabeth's imagination, and as queen she often reminded people of her status as his daughter in order to buttress her moral authority.

5 John Bale (1495–1563), a Carmelite friar who became a Protestant in the
1530s, was a zealous propagandist for the English Reformation. In 1548 he
published Elizabeth's translation of the *Mirror of the Sinful Soul*, and in dedicating
the book back to her, he praised her learning and that of her teachers: 'Blessed
be those faithful tutors and teachers which by their most godly instructions
have thus fashioned your tender youth into the right image of Christ and not
Antichrist'.

6 The burning of Anne Askewe, 16 July 1546. Despite having influential friends at Court (including Sir Anthony Denny, Chief Gentleman of the King's Privy Chamber), Anne Askew was convicted of heresy under Henry VIII's Act of Six Articles (1539), which laid down the death penalty for anyone denying the real presence of Jesus Christ in the sacrament of the altar. She was the first woman to be executed in England for Protestant beliefs. Before her execution she was tortured by Privy Councillors who hoped, in vain, to gain information from her with which to bring down Queen Catherine Parr, and who were suspicious of her evangelical sympathies and her influence over the king and his younger children.

ctio spiritus

72 Igitur da mihi domine prudenti-
am celestem. vt discam. querere. et
inuenire te, et amare te super oia.

73 Da mihi gratiam abducere et
me ab illis qui me adulantur. et
patienter illos ferre qui me adu-
vexant

74 Quando tentatio, et tribulatio su-
veniunt, digneris succurrere mihi
domine. vt omnia vertentur mihi
in spirituale solatium et semper
feram patienter. ac dicam: bene-
dictum sit nomen tuum.

fragilite laquelle tu congnois le
micubx

74 Ayes mercy de moy. et me
delyure de tout peche et iniqui-
te acellefin que ie ne soye acca
ble d'iceux

75 Il m'est souuentesfois fort gri
ef. et cela quasi me consond. de
ce que ie suis sy instable. sy fet-
ble et fragile, pour resister aux
motions iniques: lesquelles, co
bien qu'elles ne me causent de
consentir. ce nonobstant me sot
leurs assaulx tresgriefz.

7 Prayers written out by Princess Elizabeth (then aged twelve) in a little
volume she presented to her father, Henry VIII, as a New Year's gift for 1546.
Her excellent italic hand betrays the influence of the talented humanist tutors
employed by the king to teach the princess and her younger brother Edward.

8 Edward, Prince of Wales,
the future Edward VI.

9 Jane Seymour by Hans Holbein. Jane's success in bearing Henry VIII a son made her his favourite wife. They are buried together at Windsor.

10 William Cecil, Lord Burghley (1520–98), entered politics as an MP in 1542, and rose to prominence in the reign of Edward VI, serving first the Duke of Somerset and then the Duke of Northumberland, under whom he became Secretary of State. His connection with Elizabeth began around this time. Out of favour under Mary, he was with Elizabeth when news of Mary's death was brought to her. Among the queen's first acts was to appoint him her principal Secretary of State. He served her loyally as her chief minister for almost all her reign.

11 Lady Jane Grey (1537–54), eldest grand-daughter of Henry VIII's younger
sister Mary, was chosen by Edward VI as his successor. Had this plan worked,
then not only Mary Tudor but also Elizabeth would have been excluded from
the succession. Once Mary had triumphed, Jane was consigned to the Tower of
London. She was executed in the panic which followed Wyatt's Rebellion in
1554, and her noble bearing earned her widespread sympathy.

The burning of M. Iohn Rogers, vicar of Saint Pulchers, and Reader of Paules in London.

12 The burning of John Rogers, 4 February 1555, the first victim under the heresy laws recently reintroduced by Mary.

13 Philip II of Spain, engraving by F. Hogenberg, 1555. This portrait shows the prince as a young man after he had married Mary Tudor but before his father's abdication. So he is described in the frame as King of England but as Prince of Spain.

Pr^s mightie Princesse MARIE by y^e
Grace of God Queene of England.
France and Ireland &c.
From Delaram sculp Cumpton Holland exc.

14 *Above*: London Bridge. Unable to
force London Bridge on 3 February
1554, the rebel Sir Thomas Wyatt
and his Kentish followers had to
go upstream to Kingston in order
the cross the Thames (6 February).
Note the heads of traitors displayed
on poles at the gate of the city, a
familiar sight in Tudor times.

15 *Left*: Portrait engraving of
Mary, Queen of England. This late
engraving captures not so much the
tragic queen and frustrated wife as
the Tudor toughness which brought
her to the throne against the odds in
July 1553.

D.Cranmer.

D.Cole.

The description of Doctour Cranmer, howe he was plucked downe from the stage, by Friers and Papifts, for the true Confeffion of hvs Faith.

Lord receive my fpirit.

The burning of the Archbiſhop of Canturbury, Doctor Thomas Cranmer, in the Towne-ditch at Oxford, with his hand firſt thruſt into the fire, wherewith he fubfcribed before.

16. The political flexibility and frequent perjuries of Thomas Cranmer won him few friends outside the narrow circle of zealous evangelical reformers. Mary Tudor bore him particular hatred for his part in her mother's downfall. She spared him the penalty of treason in order to save him for the penalty of heresy (in her view a more heinous crime). It was probably on her specific instructions that Cranmer, despite his detailed and desperate recantations, was denied the mercy customarily shown in England to heretics who retracted their beliefs at their first offence. Finding that he was doomed to die in any case, he withdrew his recantations and at the stake dramatically plunged the hand that had signed them into the rising flames.

17 The Tower of London, where Lady Jane Grey was immured from July 1553 until her execution in February 1554. Next month the Tower welcomed its most illustrious prisoner that century, Princess Elizabeth herself.

18 Great Seal of Elizabeth I. Beneath her feet is a plinth with the motto 'Pulchrum pro patria pati' ('it is sweet to suffer for one's country'), perhaps an allusion to her experiences under Mary, which were recorded as 'virtual martyrdom' in Foxe's 'Book of Martyrs'.

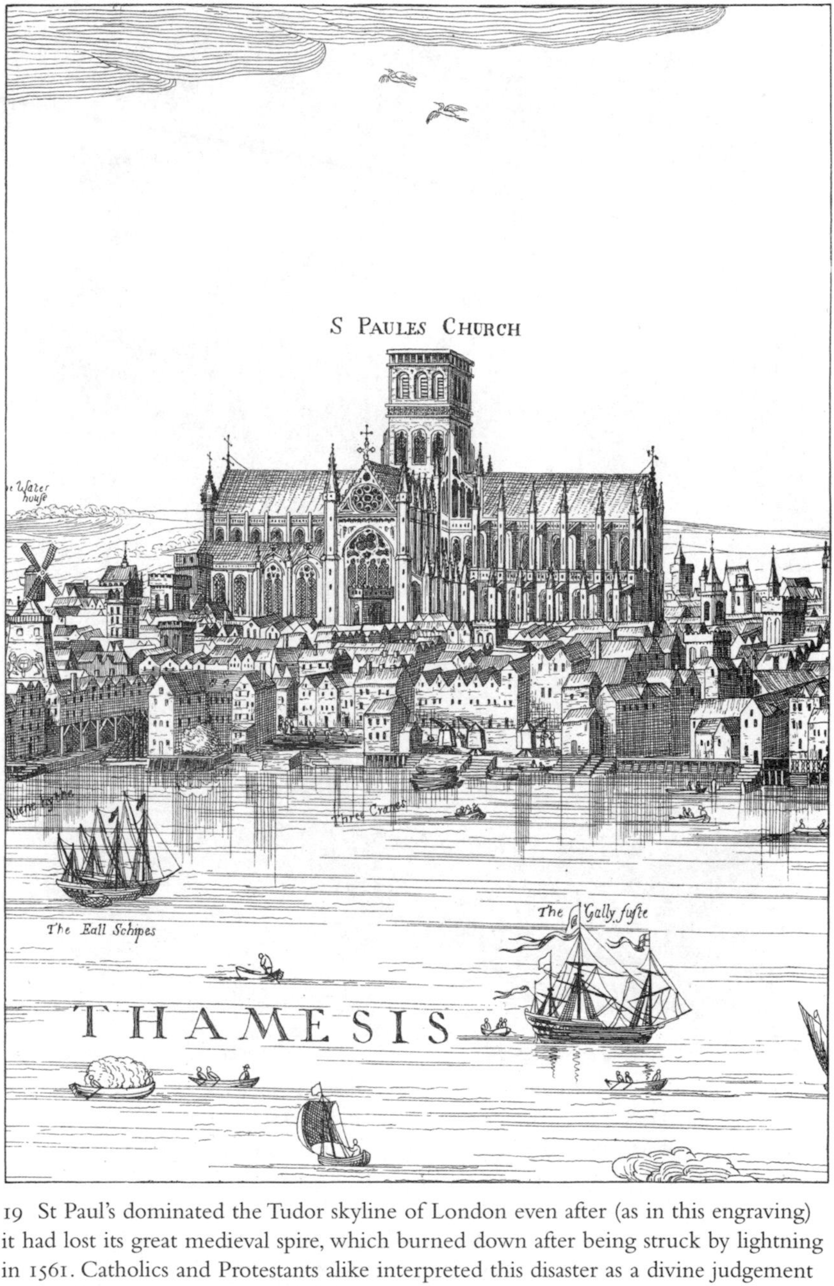
S PAULES CHURCH
Three Cranes
The Eall Schipes
The Gally fuste
THAMESIS

19 St Paul's dominated the Tudor skyline of London even after (as in this engraving) it had lost its great medieval spire, which burned down after being struck by lightning in 1561. Catholics and Protestants alike interpreted this disaster as a divine judgement against the errors and crimes of their opponents.

20 Robert Dudley, Earl of Leicester, by F. Hogenberg. Robert Dudley was a
favourite of the queen's from the start of the reign, and was given the prestigious
Court position of Master of the Horse. In the early 1560s Elizabeth was widely
reckoned to be in love with him, even though he was already married. Although
his wife died in 1560, the suspicion that her death was too timely to be an
accident made any idea of a royal marriage impossible. As a Privy Councillor he
was a close and loyal servant for many years, and he was by her side at Tilbury in
1588 as the commander of her army. He died shortly afterwards.

21 Edwin Sandys (1516–88), who would have known William Cecil at St John's College, Cambridge, in the 1530s, was another member of the circle of Cambridge graduates who dominated the early Elizabethan Church of England. Successively Bishop of Worcester and London, then Archbishop of York, he preached several times in the queen's presence.

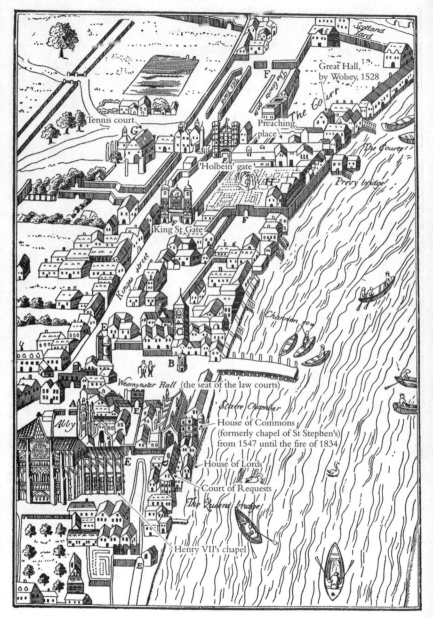

Scotland land

Great Hall,
by Wolsey, 1528

Tennis court
G

Preaching
place

'Holbein' gate
F
H

The Court

Prevy bridge

The Court

King St Gate

F

Knigs street

Charion row

F

C

B

Wesmynster Hall (the seat of the law courts)

A

Abby

E

Starre Chamber

House of Commons
(formerly chapel of St Stephen's)
from 1547 until the fire of 1834

House of Lords

Court of Requests

The Quenes bridge

E

Henry VII's chapel

E

22 Plan of the palaces of Westminster and Whitehall, from a later version of the
1578 map known as Ralph Agas's map (but not in fact by him). The Thames
was in effect the main highway connecting London, Westminster, Lambeth,
Southwark and Greenwich.

The Entrance of Q. Elizabeth.

23 The Entrance of Queen Elizabeth. Queen Elizabeth's accession (or 'entrance') came to be celebrated as a religious festival. This allegorical representation of the accession, from a later work commemorating God's mercies to Protestant England, depicts the new queen bringing justice and piety (represented by the sword and the bible) to her realm.

Yea, because of the house of the Lord our God, I will seeke to do Thee good, Pf. 122. 9.

Blessed my that Preacher bee, That will pray and speake for mee.

24 Preaching at Paul's Cross, London. Londoners flocked to hear sermons at the open-air pulpit in the cathedral churchyard. On Sunday 24 November 1588, a stately procession escorted Elizabeth to the cathedral for an official service of thanksgiving for victory over the Armada, which included a sermon preached from this pulpit by John Piers, Bishop of Salisbury.

25 Alexander Nowell (1507–1602), Dean of St Paul's, and author of what was in effect the official catechism of the Elizabethan Church of England. Nowell felt more than once the lash of the queen's tongue. When in 1565 he preached in her presence against images and idolatry (implicitly rebuking her retention of the crucifix in her private chapel), she interrupted him and instructed him sharply to drop that subject and get back to his text. Yet on another occasion, when he sought to please her by presenting her with a finely illustrated prayer book, she cast the accusation of idolatry back in his teeth, spurning his gift.

The burning of Tho.Tomkins hand by B.Boner,who not long after burnt alſo his body.

26 Edmund Bonner (Bishop of London, 1539–59) as Protestants saw him thanks to John *Foxe's Acts and Monuments* (often known as his 'Book of Martyrs'). Here he is shown tormenting a captive Protestant by applying a candle to his hand. As around sixty out of nearly 300 Protestant martyrs under Queen Mary were burned in London, Bonner understandably held a prominent place in Protestant demonology. Yet he was also active in some of the more positive aspects of the restoration of Catholicism, and in 1559 he led Catholic resistance to Elizabeth's alteration of religion. He was consigned to the Marshalsea prison, where he died in 1569.

27 *Above*: Two pages from the Book of Common Prayer, 1559. The words given here for the administration of communion (right-hand page) combine the formula of 1549 with that of the Second Edwardine Prayer Book, 1552, deliberately introducing an element of ambiguity about the Prayer Book's theology of Christ's eucharistic presence.

28 *Opposite*: Title-page of the first Marprelate Tract. The first of the Martin Marprelate pamphlets was the introductory *Epistle* printed at East Mousley in reply to Dr Bridges, Dean of Salisbury. It was followed by the promised *Epitome*, and both were published in 1588. The wickedly witty and subversive Marprelate Tracts were a massive embarrassment to the establishment until the clandestine press was tracked down and silenced. The 'John Penry' whose name is added here was involved in the production of the tracts, although the main author was Job Throckmorton. When he came under suspicion, Penry fled to Scotland in 1590. Unwisely returning to England late in 1592, he was swiftly dispatched on trumped-up charges of treason in 1593.

Oh read ouer D. John Bridges/ for it is a worthy worke:

❧ Or an epitome of the

fyrste Booke/ of that right worshipfull vo-
lume/ written against the Puritanes/ in the defence of
the noble cleargie/ by as worshipfull a prieste/ Iohn Bridges/
Presbyter/Priest or elder/doctor of Diuillitie/ and Deane of
Sarum.Wherein the arguments of the puritans are
wisely preuented/ that when they come to an-
swere M. Doctor/ they must needes
say something that hath
bene spoken.

Compiled for the behoofe and overthrow of
the Parsons/Fyckers/and Currats/that haue lernt
their Catechismes/and are past grace: By the reuerend
and worthie Martin Marprelate gentleman/and
dedicated to the Confocationhouse.

The Epitome is not yet published/ but it shall be when
the Bishops are at conuenient leysure to view the same.
In the meane time/let them be content with
this learned Epistle.

or ap Henry
by John Penry ✳ woodd Athis Boor Vi P. 260

Printed oversea/ in Europe/ within two fur-
longs of a Bounsing Priest/at the cost and charges
of M. Marprelate/gentleman.

29 John Knox from a 1580 woodcut. The awesome prophet of the Scottish Reformation is sporting the patriarchal beard which from about 1550 became fashionable among Protestant ministers as a way of distinguishing themselves from the tonsured and generally clean-shaven priesthood of the Catholic Church. Elizabeth never forgave him for his *First Blast of the Trumpet against the Monstrous Regiment of Women* (Geneva, 1558).

30, 31 Illustrations from George Gascoigne, *The Noble Arte of Venerie or Hunting* (1575), pp.90 and 133. Above, Elizabeth enjoys a picnic during a hunt. Below, the huntsman presents Elizabeth with a knife to make the first cut in butchering the deer.

32 Elizabeth's falcon downs a heron. Illustration from George Turberville, *The Book of Faulconrie* or *Hauking* (1575), p.81. The books of Gascoigne and Turberville were issued as a pair and are usually found bound within a single cover. Alhough neither book explicitly states that the princely lady in the illustratrations is meant to be Queen Elizabeth, the Tudor roses on the liveried servants in the scenes makes her identity obvious.

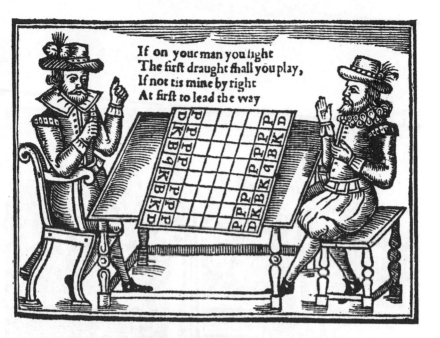

If on your man you light
The firft draught fhall you play,
If not tis mine by right
At firft to lead the way

33 *Above*: Elizabeth enjoyed playing both chess and draughts, although her successor, James I, thought chess 'over-wise and Philosophique folly... it filleth and troubleth mens heades with as many fashious toyes of the play, as before it was filled with thoughts on his affaires'. This illustration is taken from Arthur Saul's *The Famous Game of Chesse-Play* (1614), which describes the game as 'an exercise full of delight; fit for princes'.

34 *Left*: George Gascoigne depicted presenting a book to Queen Elizabeth. She is seated in her Chamber of Presence on a throne beneath a 'cloth of estate', a formal sign of her royal status.

Raro antecedentem Scelestum:

Campian

B. Parsons & Campian   I.H. fecit

Rebellion the effect of Monasteries.

35 Parsons and Campion from George Carleton, *A Thankfull Remembrance of Gods Mercy in the Deliverance of the Church and State in the reigns of Elizabeth and James I*, 1627. Although Edmund Campion and Robert Parsons were not the first of a new breed of Catholic missionary to come to minister to the remaining English Catholics, their secret arrival in 1580 soon became public knowledge, and their whirlwind ministry lifted Catholic morale and panicked the Protestant authorities. Every effort was made to track them down, and while Parsons escaped to the Continent, Campion was captured at Stonor Park (Oxfordshire) in 1581. After torture and a state trial, he was executed for treason on 1 December. Denounced by government pamphleteers for a traitor (as in this picture), he was venerated by Catholics, and eventually canonised, as a martyr.

A View of the House of Peers, Queen Elizabeth on the Throne, the Commons attending.
Taken from a Painted Print in the Cottonian Library.

Cancellary seats

Prolocuter

Milites Provinciarum et Burgenses (quos vocant) atq; qui Cameram Parliamenti inferiorem constituunt Prolocutorem conducentes.

The Knights of Shires & Burgesses (as they call them) which constitute ŷ lower house of Parliament, presenting their Speaker.

36 Queen Elizabeth presiding in the House of Lords at the opening of
parliament. In the foreground the Commons stand at the Bar and present their
Speaker.

37 The Red Cross Knight from Edmund Spenser's *The Faerie Queen* (3rd edition, 1598). This vast chivalric epic, one of the supreme artistic achievements of the cult of Queen Elizabeth, was designed as an allegory of the political and religious struggle between Protestantism and Catholicism.

Marie Stuart

38 Three unhappy marriages, to an immature boy (King Francis I of France),
a feckless youth (Henry Lord Darnley), and a reckless adventurer (James Earl
Bothwell), made Mary Queen of Scots an object lesson to Elizabeth in the risks of
sexual passion and marriage.

39 End of a letter from Mary Queen of Scots to Elizabeth, asking to be allowed a Catholic chaplain while in captivity. As she had been brought up in France since the age of six, French was her language of choice.

40 The Royal Exchange, founded by Sir Thomas Gresham in 1564. He laid the foundation on 7 June 1566. On 23 January 1571, Elizabeth I visited the building and had it proclaimed the Royal Exchange. This visit is a typical example of her skill in public relations. The royal visit was itself a display of favour, and her concession of 'Royal' status to the Exchange gratified both Gresham and the London mercantile community.

41 Roman Catholic plots against Elizabeth, as seen in part of an engraving by Cornelius Danckwerts, entitled *A Thankfull Remembrance of Gods Mercie*, which was issued to accompany the 1625 edition of George Carleton's book of the same title. At the top: Dr Lopez, Elizabeth's physician, who was executed in 1590 having been convicted on scanty evidence of attempting to poison the queen. In the central panel: Pope Pius V, who excommunicated Elizabeth on 25 February 1570, releasing her subjects from all oaths of allegiance to her, shown here with the Earls of Northumberland and Westmoreland, whose rebellion had in fact been suppressed before the papal bull was published; Don John of Austria, to whom the crown of Ireland was offered in 1577 by James Fitzgerald, one of the family of the Earl of Desmond; Sir Thomas Stukeley, who secured papal and Spanish support for a campaign in Ireland; and the Earl of Desmond, whose tenants and clansmen forced him into revolt in 1579. At the bottom: the Babington Plot, which aimed at the assassination of Elizabeth and her replacement by Mary Queen of Scots.

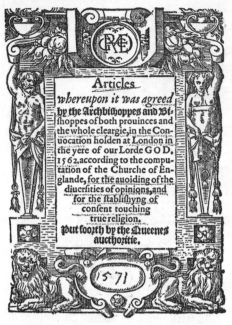

Articles
*whereupon it was agreed
by the Archbishoppes and Bishoppes of both prouinces and
the whole cleargie, in the Conuocation holden at London in
the yere of our Lorde GOD,
1562, according to the computation of the Churche of Englande, for the auoiding of the
diuersities of opinions, and
for the stablishyng of
consent touching
true religion.
Put foorth by the Queenes
authoritie.*

1571

42 Title-page of the 'Thirty-Nine Articles', 1571. The Thirty-Nine Articles were drafted at Convocation in 1563 on the basis of Cranmer's Forty-Two Articles of 1553. Their final form was fixed by Convocation in 1571, and authorised by an Act of Parliament of that year, which required all clergy serving in the Church of England to subscribe to the articles. This requirement was relaxed in 1865, and reduced to virtual meaninglessness in 1975.

Anno xxvii. Reginæ Elizabethæ.

¶ At the Parliament
*begunne and holden at Westminster,
the xxiij. day of Nouember, in the
xxvii. yeere of the reigne of our most
gracious Soueraigne Lady Elizabeth, by the
grace of God, of England, France, and Ireland Queene, defender of the Faith, &c.
and there continued, vntill the
xxix. of March following:*

To the high pleasure of Almightie God,
and the weale publike of this
Realme, were enacted
as followeth.

*Imprinted at London by Christopher
Barker, Printer to the Queenes most excellent Maiestie.*

1585.

43 Acts of Parliament, 1585. A practice introduced under Richard III and followed under all the Tudors was to print the new Acts of Parliament passed at the end of each session. This is the title page of the sessional print for the parliament which sat from November 1584 until March 1585. The first act in this book was one making provision 'for the surety of the Queen's person'. It followed up the Bond of Association which had circulated earlier in 1584, providing legal and political remedies in the event of plots against the queen, and in particular in the event of her assassination.

44 Francis Walsingham (1532–90) entered Elizabeth's service in the 1560s. As ambassador to France (1571–72) he witnessed the Massacre of St Bartholomew's Day in Paris (1572), and returned to England consumed with fear and hatred of Catholicism. He built up a formidable network of spies and informers at home and abroad, without which Elizabeth might well have fallen victim to one of the many plots against her.

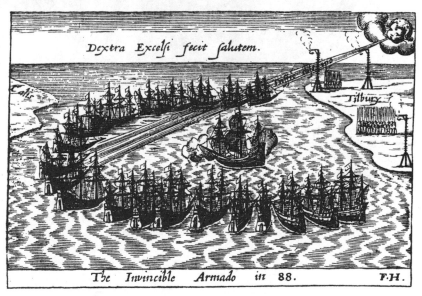

Dextra Excelsi fecit salutem.

The Invincible Armado in 88.   F·H·

45 The Spanish Armada off the French coast. From George Carleton's *Thankfull Remembrance* (1627). By the 1620s, when this pamphlet was published, the 'Protestant wind' here shown blowing along the Channel was already a fixture in the national mythology.

FERDINANDVS ALVARES TOLETANVS. DVX. ALVÆ. MARCHIO. CORIÆ &. SALVATERRÆ &c. BELGICAR. PHILIP. II. REGIS HISPAN. PROVINC: GVBERNAT: EIVSQ EXERCITVS CAPITANEVS GENERALIS

46 Fernando Alvarez de Toledo, Duke of Alva (1507–82), was sent as Governor General to the Netherlands in 1567 with the task of suppressing the burgeoning religious and nationalist discontent there. He crushed rebellion pitilessly in 1568, executing about 1,000 people. In the early 1570s, Philip II wanted him to send troops to England to support Roberto Ridolfi's conspiracy to put Mary Queen of Scots on the throne, but the plot was uncovered long before this dream could become a reality. A second rebellion in the Netherlands in 1572 resulted in even more bloodshed, and Alva's failure to crush it utterly led to his recall to Spain in 1573.

47 'A Hieroglyphic of Britain', which John Dee himself designed as the frontispiece to his *General and Rare Memorials Pertayning to the Perfect Arte of Navigation* (1577). John Dee (1527–1608), alchemist, geographer, mathematician and astrologer to the queen, wrote the *Arte of Navigation* as a manifesto for Elizabethan naval imperialism. He explains in the text (p. 53) that the frontispiece shows the British Republic (or commonwealth) 'on her Knees, very Humbly and ernestly Soliciting the most Excellent Royall Maiesty, of our Elizabeth, (Sitting at the helm of this Imperiall Monarchy; or rather, at the helm of this Imperiall Ship, of the most parte of Christendome...)', and that above is a 'Good Angell', sent by God to guard the English people 'with Shield and Sword'. Elizabeth steers her vessel towards the Tower of Safety, atop which stands Victory, ready with a wreath to crown her.

48 Sir Francis Drake's circumnavigation of the globe and daring naval (or piratical) exploits earned him fame throughout Europe. Known to Spaniards as 'el dragón', Drake became for a time the bogeyman for the Spanish, as Napoleon ('Boney') did for nineteenth-century England.

49 Nonsuch, Henry VIII's fantasy palace, was built around 1540 out of materials recycled from suppressed monasteries. It was one of Elizabeth's favourite residences. It was here, in 1585, that England entered into an alliance with the rebel states of the Netherlands against Spain. Nonsuch fell into disuse and disrepair under the Stuarts, and Charles II used it to pay off one of his discarded mistresses, Barbara Villiers. She demolished the palace for its scrap value in 1682.

50 William 'the Silent', Prince of Orange (1533–84), the leader of the Protestant and nationalist rebels in the Netherlands. His assassination in July 1584 heightened political tensions in England. Mary Queen of Scots was placed in closer confinement, and the Bond of Association was drawn up that autumn as a demonstration of the unconditional loyalty of England's ruling elites.

Babington with his Complices in St. Giles fields.

51 In 1586, the Derbyshire gentleman Anthony Babington was the central figure in a plot to liberate Mary Queen of Scots and assassinate Elizabeth. The confidence in success which led him to commission a group portrait of the conspirators was misplaced. Sir Francis Walsingham's spies had penetrated the conspiracy and all the correspondence between the plotters and the captive queen passed across his desk. In due course Babington and the rest were rounded up. They were executed on 20 September 1586. The real significance of this plot was that it enabled the Privy Council to overcome Elizabeth's reluctance to sanction a definitive solution to the problem posed by Mary.

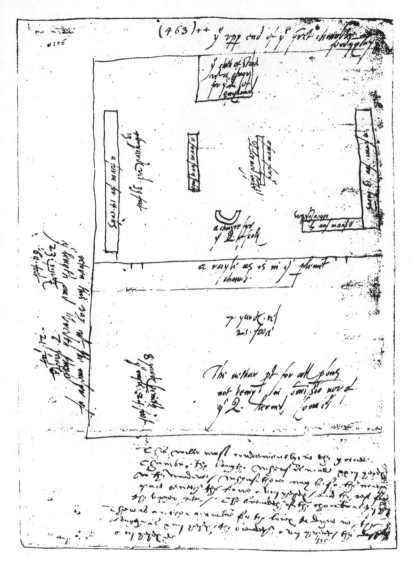

52 Rough sketch by William Cecil, Lord Burghley, of the arrangement of the hall of Fotheringay Castle for the trial of Mary Queen of Scots in October 1586. He provides seating around the walls for the earls, barons and Privy Councillors who were commissioned to try the case. Between them is a chair for 'the Queen of Scots'. Facing her is a throne beneath a cloth of estate to represent the majesty of Queen Elizabeth (who did not attend in person). Mary, under protest, was tried on 14 and 15 October, but sentence was not passed until the commissioners reconvened at Westminster on 25 October.

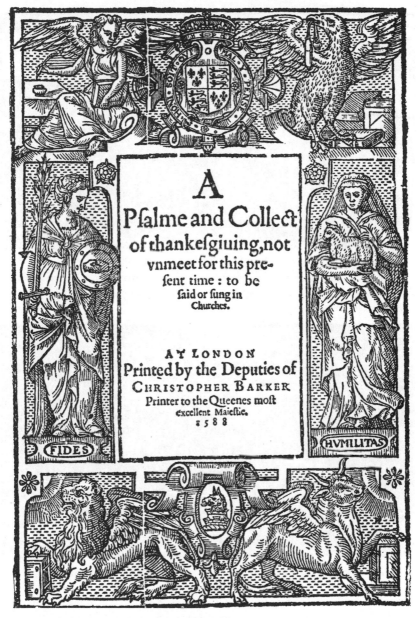

A

Pſalme and Collect

of thankeſgiuing, not
vnmeet for this pre-
ſent time : to be
ſaid or ſung in
Churches.

AT LONDON
Printed by the Deputies of
CHRISTOPHER BARKER
Printer to the Queenes moſt
excellent Maieſtie.
1588

FIDES

HVMILITAS

53 Title page of a thanksgiving service issued in 1588 for use in churches to celebrate the defeat of the Spanish Armada.

54 English troops on the march in Ireland. The Irish found little mercy at English hands. Lord Deputy Grey boasted of how, in his two years in Ireland in the early 1580s, he had executed nearly 1,500 Irishmen of some rank, besides 'innumerable' churls.

O.Sydney worthy of tryple re. nowne, For plaging tho traytours that troubled the crowne. 1581.

55 The reception of Sir Henry Sidney (Elizabeth I's Lord Deputy in Ireland) by the mayor and aldermen of Dublin, upon his return to the city after a victory over rebels. It was during Sidney's two terms of office as deputy that the English government's policy towards the Irish turned decisively towards martial law and ever more brutal repression.

56 Engraved portrait of Elizabeth I from the original portrait presented to Sir
Henry Sidney, Lord Deputy of Ireland, by Elizabeth I. Although in Mary's reign
Elizabeth had affected the simplest and plainest fashions in dress (in order to
distinguish herself from her overdressed sister and to allude to the Protestant
aesthetic of plain simplicity), once she became queen, Elizabeth re-invented
herself with the aid of spectacularly ornate dresses such as this, festooned with
small fortunes in jewellery.

Tyrones false Submission afterwards rebelling.

57 Hugh O'Neill, Earl of Tyrone, formally renewed his allegiance to Elizabeth at the hands of Lord Deputy Russell in Dublin in 1594. Nevertheless, within the year he was in rebellion, and with Spanish support went on to wage war against the queen for nine years.

58 Portrait engraving of Francis Bacon. Bacon's early advancement came thanks to the patronage of the Earl of Essex, but Essex's strenuous and tactless efforts to have him made Attorney General in 1593 offended Elizabeth I (who appointed Sir Edward Coke) and not only hampered Bacon's prospects but damaged Essex's credit.

59 This depiction of the queen is rich in political and religious symbolism. The twin columns denote imperial sovereignty, and perhaps also the command of the seas suggested in the background. The 'pious pelican' feeding her young from her own substance and the phoenix rising from the ashes are symbols of Christian faith and life, and also of the queen's selfless devotion to her realm. The open book, with its motto ('I have chosen God as my helper') reminds viewers of her commitment to the 'Word of God'. The verses beneath assure readers that peace, faith and justice will reign for ever in Britain.

60 Sir Edward Coke (1552–1634), Attorney General and Speaker of the House of Commons under Elizabeth I and James I. As Attorney General he prosecuted charges of treason against the Earl of Essex, Sir Walter Raleigh, and the Gunpowder Plot conspirators. His entirely artificial moral indignation against the 'equivocation' of the Jesuit Henry Garnet at his trial in 1606 presents an ironic contrast with his own readiness to tell flat lies in court.

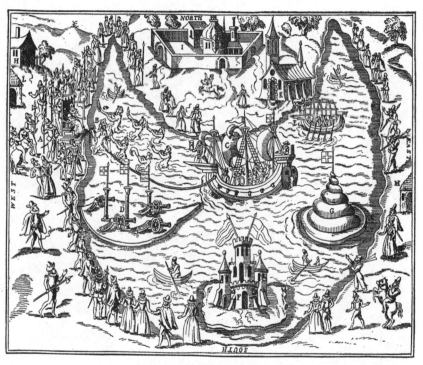

61 When Elizabeth visited the Earl of Hertford at Elvetham in 1591, he arranged splendid outdoor entertainments around a small ornamental lake in the shape of a half-moon, specially dug for the occasion. The entertainments, including pageants, songs, verses, fireworks and banquets, filled the all three days of her visit. In this picture of the scene, Elizabeth is shown seated beside the left horn of the moon on a throne beneath a cloth of estate.

62 Portrait of Richard Tarlton. Tarlton was introduced to Elizabeth I through
the Earl of Leicester and became immensely popular as one of the Queen's
Players, specialising in the dramatic jigs popular at the time.

63 The 'Procession Picture'.

64 The earliest depiction of the State barge, in a royal procession by water. The thistle and royal arms of England on the banner and drapery of the principal barge are probably the insignia of James I, but the fashion of these vessels remained unchanged from the time of Elizabeth I.

The Bear Gardne

The Globe

65 The Bear Garden and the Globe Theatre from Visscher's Panorama of London. Southwark, across the Thames from London, was a jurisdictional 'liberty', immune from both the City of London and the Surrey county authorities. A flourishing red-light district, it was the natural home for bear-pits and playhouses.

increasingly threadbare. Yet, to be fair, repression was imposed upon her almost as much as upon her Catholic subjects. The Catholics held Cecil chiefly to blame for their miseries, and although in early modern Europe there was a polite preference for blaming ministers rather than monarchs, for once there is much to suggest that they were right. Cecil's papers for the 1580s and 1590s are full of bright ideas for tightening the screws on Catholics, from imposing the oath of supremacy on laymen to taking away the children of recusants for re-education. The 1571 bill which Elizabeth vetoed was powerfully urged in the Commons by Thomas Norton, one of Cecil's closest political allies, and in the Lords by Cecil himself. It might be thought that Elizabeth was simply diverting the flak for this policy onto Cecil, as she diverted the flak for the repression of Puritans onto her Archbishops of Canterbury. Yet while we have good evidence for her role in commanding her bishops to act against the Puritans, the evidence with regard to the Catholics points in the other direction. Elizabeth's ministers were the driving force, led by Cecil and egged on by Francis Walsingham (appointed Secretary in 1573), whose profoundly anti-Catholic attitudes were shaped by his experience as ambassador in Paris, where he had witnessed the horrors of the Massacre of St

Bartholomew's Day. They even manipulated the information which was supplied to her in order to build up the Catholic threat as far as they could. Only thus could they induce her to implement even a selection of the imaginative sanctions they worked out. It is to Elizabeth's credit that the more inhumane schemes were kept off the statute book. And it says something for the way she was seen that Catholics more than once petitioned her for toleration. Protestants under Mary had never for one moment thought it worth addressing such a petition to her. This is not to set up Elizabeth as some sort of model of toleration. Had she wished to grant toleration to Catholics, there was little to stop her. Her demand for outward obedience to her religious settlement was uncompromising. But she was more sensitive than her chief minister to the accusation of persecuting men for their religion.

Although most Catholic victims suffered under laws which simply redefined their religion as treason, the widespread fear of 'popery' was by no means groundless. The later sixteenth and early seventeenth centuries saw a series of high-profile political assassinations, usually of Protestants by Catholics, sometimes of Catholics by Catholics: Admiral Gaspard de Coligny in 1572, Prince William of Orange in

1584, Duke Henry of Guise and Cardinal Charles de Guise in 1588, Henri III of France in 1589, and Henry IV of France in 1610. Add to this that some Catholic theologians were prepared to justify tyrannicide, and there was genuine reason to fear for the queen's safety. Catholic plots against her were regularly brought to light by Walsingham, who had built up a formidable network of spies and informers. However, few Catholics participated in the plots. Most Catholics bent over backwards with a disconcerting spinelessness designed to put their loyalty to the person of Elizabeth beyond any doubt: a testimony to the power of the Tudor myth, and to the growing symbolic power of the English State (it is towards the end of Elizabeth's reign that the term 'State' begins to be used in English in something approaching its modern political sense). In 1585, Catholic loyalists petitioned the queen, in vain, in these terms:

> We do protest before the living God that all and every priest and priests, who have at any time conversed with us, have recognised your Majesty their lawful and undoubted queen... And if we knew or shall know in any of them one point of treason or treacherous device or any undecent speech... we do bind ourselves

by oath irrevocable to be the first appre-
henders and accusers of such.

At the time of the Armada, a group of Catholic
noblemen approached the government and
offered, in return for the relaxation of recusancy
fines, to raise, equip and maintain in the field at
their own expense a troop of horsemen for the
defence of the realm. Under the circumstances,
Cecil was predictably reluctant to authorise the
formation of a Catholic private army, and was
strongly opposed in principle to any relaxation
of the penal laws, so the offer was rejected. But
when he composed the official account of the
defeat of the Armada, he gleefully included the
whole story in order to emphasise to Catholics
abroad the total loyalty of the Tudor queen's
subjects (even while insisting at home on the
intrinsic treachery of those same Catholic subjects in order to justify the penal system with
which he kept a grip on them).

The increasing pressure on Catholics in the
later 1570s and '80s was imposed upon the queen
on account of the worsening international situation, which was to culminate in open war
between England and Spain. This was certainly
not a conflict that Elizabeth wanted. As with so
much in her life, her actions were driven by cir-
cumstance, and policies were forced upon her.

The emerging conflict itself was not primarily a religious war, yet the religious gulf between Catholic Spain and Protestant England was what drove the reorientation of English foreign policy by which a new enmity with Spain was substituted for the traditional enmity with France. It was the combination of this religious division and the clash of interests between England and Spain in the Netherlands (and to a lesser extent on the high seas) that led inexorably to conflict.

Philip II of Spain had serious problems in the Netherlands, one of his hereditary territories, where Lutheran, Anabaptist and Calvinist brands of Protestant Reformation had by the 1560s made significant inroads among one of Europe's most urbanised and educated populations. Of course, Catholicism also retained a very considerable following. But the fragmented nature of local political authority in the Netherlands often impeded effective repression of religious dissent (except when backed by overwhelming and expensive military force), with the result that at many times there was almost a free market in religion. Philip wished to eliminate religious diversity in the province. Any sustained attempt to do this was likely to be bad for trade as well as for Protestantism, and English interests in the

Netherlands were primarily in trade, and secondly in solidarity with their Protestant coreligionists. Refugees from the Netherlands were often allowed to settle in England, where 'strangers' churches' (churches providing worship according to foreign rites) were sometimes made available to them.

While English attempts to muscle in on Atlantic trade in the 1560s led to distant battles with Spanish vessels, these marine equivalents of border incidents, involving privateers rather than the queen's navy, did not seriously upset relations between the two kingdoms. However, the seizure of Spanish bullion in December 1568, when treasure ships *en route* for the Netherlands had to take refuge at Southampton from storms and pirates, might at other moments have been tantamount to a declaration of war. This sudden move, indeed false move, is somewhat out of keeping with Cecil's usual caution and Elizabeth's habitual hesitation. Cecil, who was mostly responsible, was driven by a deep-seated suspicion of Spain arising from his strongly anti-papal (if theologically simple, even naïve) version of Protestantism. Elizabeth's consent, if indeed it was properly obtained before the treasure was taken ashore, seems to have been motivated more by the prospect of easy money. As the bullion had not yet been delivered to the Netherlands, it could still in some sense be regarded as the property of the Genoese bankers who were lending it to Philip II, so her government was in a strong position to negotiate a loan on favourable terms. The Spanish reacted quickly, perhaps over-reacted, by impounding English ships, and trade between England and the Netherlands broke down. In the event, things did not turn out as badly for England as they might have done. Trade returned to normal in about a year, and while the evident hostility of the English government led to Spanish complicity in the Northern Rising of 1569, and the plots focusing on Mary Queen of Scots, the financial costs inflicted on both sides did long-term damage only to the Spanish in the Netherlands. The Duke of Alva's mission to 'pacify' the Netherlands was hampered at a crucial moment by the English coup.

The contacts of the Spanish ambassador with the rebel earls in 1569, and his involvement in the Ridolfi Plot the following year, led to his dismissal from Court and return home. Diplomatic relations between the two countries ceased for a few years. Again, this damaged Spain more than England. More disaffected subjects of Philip took refuge in England from the Netherlands, among them pirates who harried Spanish shipping in the Channel. Ironically, it was an English decision in 1572 to curtail their hospitality to these 'Sea Beggars' that led them to raid Brill in search of a base back on their home territory – an event which sparked off rebellion throughout Holland and Zeeland. Philip's problems with the Netherlands had moved onto a new and more troubling level. Despite Elizabeth's protestations of sympathy with the Spanish predicament – as ever, she had a gut reaction against any kind of rebellion – many of the Dutch refugees in England were permitted to rush home to join the rising. For the rest of the decade, Elizabeth and her ministers could enjoy the spectacle of successive Spanish governors floundering in the murky waters of Dutch politics, while the Protestant Reformation, in the form of Dutch Calvinism (sufficiently close to the Church of England in theology, although not in church government) made headway. Meanwhile, English privateers harried and plundered Spain's Atlantic shipping.

Spain's problems in the Netherlands were an open invitation to France, which had for centuries striven to expand into the confusing patchwork of civic privileges and feudal principalities which lay on her northern borders. For a brief moment, some of Elizabeth's advisers even contemplated an offensive alliance with France against Spanish interests there, as in their turn the young King of France, Charles IX, and his mother, Catherine de Medici, flirted with the Huguenot princes and nobles with a view to reducing the power of the Guise dynasty. The brief moment passed when the flirtation turned unexpectedly into a bloodbath. At the instigation of Catherine de Medici, the Huguenot leaders were assassinated at the French Court in the 'Massacre of St Bartholomew's Day' (24 August 1572), and the Catholic people of France, following the royal lead, butchered Huguenots in towns and cities across the country.

The massacre was one of the decisive moments in English as well as French history. It probably shocked English Protestants even more than the rising of the Northern Earls in 1569, and it vindicated the very worst suspicions and fears of the bloodthirstiness and untrustworthiness of 'papists'. There were, inevitably, renewed calls for the execution of Mary Queen of Scots. Spanish repression of Protestants in the Netherlands and Catholic massacres of Huguenots in France now looked very much like a conspiracy, and minds harked back to the meeting of Catherine de Medici with the Duke of Alva at Bayonne in 1565. The Protestant imagination was particularly open to the apocalyptic, and this was the kind of thing they expected to herald the end of the world. More to the point, it heralded a new phase in the civil wars of France. Spain could act in the Netherlands with less fear of French interference. The cause of the Reformation was under threat, and many in England saw it as their mission to succour their co-religionists abroad. In seeking to understand the English Protestantism of Elizabeth's reign (though not that of Elizabeth herself), it is crucial to realise that the bishops and theologians of the Church of England identified their cause with that of continental Calvinism, even if Elizabeth was far from agreeing with them.

The paradox of Elizabethan diplomacy in the 1570s was the need to maintain, as far as possible, good relations with the Catholic power which had perpetrated the massacre, while simultaneously maintaining good relations with the Huguenots. England's only card, now looking a little dog-eared, was the queen's marriage. The suggestion was that she might marry Francis, the youngest brother of the French king. Francis, Duke of Alençon and later (once his elder brother Henri became Henri III of France in 1576) Duke of Anjou, came closer than anyone else to securing Elizabeth's hand in marriage. It is still difficult to believe that Elizabeth ever had any intention of going through with it, but, as Spanish fortunes in the Netherlands revived in the later 1570s, under the vigorous general-ship of Alessandro Farnese, Duke of Parma and Piacenza, the political value of friendship with France drove the negotiations on.

Political opposition to the Anjou match in England made Mary Tudor's marriage to Philip of Spain look popular. Pamphlets were published against it, argued in violent and apocalyptic terms. To the fear of a foreign prince was now added fanatical hatred of his religion. The best-known opponent of the marriage is John Stubbs, whose *Discovery of a Gaping Gulf* laid out the arguments in lucid and lurid terms. Elizabeth had reacted furiously on previous occasions when the gentry of the House of Commons had dared debate her marriage and the succession in the relative privacy of parliament, regarding even this interference as an infringement of her prerogative. Her reaction to the colossal impertinence of being told what to do, in public, by a Puritan commoner from Norfolk, was savage. Stubbs and his printer were prosecuted under a statute from the previous reign, and were sentenced to lose their right hands. The silence of the crowd as this sentence was executed – Stubbs bravely waved his stump and shouted 'Long live the queen' before fainting from shock – was widely interpreted as a vote of sympathy for the victim. The

Spanish ambassador thought the people would rise up if the marriage went ahead. His knowledge of the people may have been restricted to London, but London mattered. As some lawyers reckoned the statute under which Stubbs's sentence was imposed was no longer in force, and as the arguments which Stubbs deployed reflected remarkably closely those being urged against the marriage by members of the Privy Council, the impetus behind the prosecution and the execution of this cruel punishment can only have come from the queen herself – a rare false move from a woman who was so skilled in public relations.

Mary Tudor's Council had at least been decently divided over her marriage. Elizabeth's was almost unanimous in its disapproval. The only exception was the Earl of Sussex, a councillor of the old guard, who did not share the hatred and fear of 'popery' which consumed most of his colleagues. He had always wanted to see Elizabeth married and the succession secured, and when you had as many Catholic relatives as he did, you were not scared by the prospect of a Catholic king. However, while Elizabeth relied upon his unshakeable loyalty (it was he to whom she had entrusted the suppression of the rebellion in 1569), she was not overly attentive to his opinion. The Anjou match reached its crisis in 1579, when Anjou was granted the privilege, rare among her hopeful foreign suitors, of an invitation to England and to Court. In fact, Anjou came and left in August without a cast-iron decision, but with the distinct impression that the queen was favourable. Yet it remains hard to see Elizabeth's display of enthusiasm for the marriage as anything other than a ploy. Anjou was an ugly and ungainly little man. Though she treated him with every sign of affection during his visit, he was simply not her type – she liked handsome, dashing, athletic men like Leicester, Hatton, Raleigh and Essex.

The intricate politics of Elizabeth's change of heart will be endlessly debated. But it seems likely that, in a move typical of her governmental technique, she wanted to shift the blame for her own unwillingness to marry onto her councillors. She wanted them to beg her not to marry Anjou, before graciously conceding in a way which would make it their fault, not hers, that she had never married. In the event, they called her bluff. Shortly after Anjou's departure, they undertook, despite their misgivings, to do their best to implement her will. By the New Year, she was backing away from the marriage, and her councillors and ambassadors were busy disengaging her from whatever commitments she might be thought to have entered into.

Queen and Council had stared each other out, and the queen had blinked first. In fact, negotiations were kept open for a year or two, and Anjou made a second visit to England in the hope of rescuing his blighted prospects. But whatever favour Elizabeth might show him was discounted in her private dealings with her councillors, who now knew that she had no intention of going through with it, and helped her play the game to its conclusion – Anjou's departure, with some suitable financial compensation, in February 1582

VIII

WAR WITH SPAIN:
1580–1588

It was only towards the end of the 1570s that the cold war between England and Spain started to heat up. Spanish resurgence in the Netherlands from 1578 onwards was bad enough, but worse was to come. In 1580 the direct line of succession to the throne of Portugal expired, and on a long shortlist of potential heirs, Philip II probably had the best claim. There was a Portuguese candidate, but he was a bastard, and it was difficult at that time for the illegitimate to appeal to *légitimisme*. Overwhelming force secured the succession for Philip, and thus brought under his control the vast financial resources of Portugal's trade and overseas empire. With fresh resources came fresh ambition, and Philip's agents plotted in Rome, France and England with Elizabeth's disaffected Catholic subjects and with the militantly Catholic Guise faction in France. Vast strategic schemes were devised for the invasion of first Scotland and then England, with a view to substituting Mary Queen of Scots for Elizabeth. At home in England, plans to assassinate Elizabeth were unmasked with a regularity that was at times suspicious. But Francis Walsingham's network of informers and double-agents served him well, even if they often crossed the boundary between detection and entrapment.

Elizabeth in her turn gave ever more open support to the war at sea being waged by privateers such as Francis Drake, whom she knighted on board the Golden Hind, moored on the Thames, in April 1581 upon his return, laden with Spanish booty, from his circumnavigation of the globe. With English aid to the Portuguese pretender, Don Antonio, and Spanish aid to rebels in Ireland, the two countries drifted towards a war which almost everyone saw as inevitable. The new ways of the world were signalled in the absence of any formal declaration of war. Yet when Drake sailed for the West Indies in autumn 1585 with a fleet of over twenty ships, he did so under a commission from the queen which made his expedition an act of war.

The Dutch had for some time been angling for more than moral support from England, and the fall of Antwerp to Farnese in 1585 brought the situation to a critical point for Elizabeth's government. Despite her misgivings about war, her councillors prevailed upon her to intervene directly. Under a treaty signed in August at Nonsuch Palace, the Earl of Leicester led a force of several thousand men to assist Philip's enemies in the Netherlands. This represented an important shift in policy for the queen. Since the ill-fated expedition to Le Havre in 1562-63, she had held out against invitations or advice to send troops into foreign theatres. As a queen, she had little enough to gain from war. Kings and nobles, educated in and motivated by a tradition of chivalry and martial prowess, could seek glory in conquest, in battle, even up to a point in defeat. For all the cynicism of More's *Utopia*, and for all the pacifism of a fashionable intellectual like Erasmus in his widely read essay on the proverb 'dulce bellum inexpertis' ('war is sweet – if you're not in it'), the space which sixteenth-century chronicles still gave to detailed accounts of military preparations and actions reminds us that for many men of that time, war was in effect the highest form of politics. Once kings went to war, cost was no object (although at times it might become an insuperable obstacle, as it had for Henry VIII in 1525). Elizabeth had a very clear sense of the cost, and a shrewd sense that such benefits as there might be would mostly redound elsewhere. She hesitated long before agreeing to go to war (there had been pressure for this since the later 1570s). And she hesitated long before appointing Leicester to lead the expedition.

The Earl of Leicester might have been genuinely committed to the protection of Dutch Calvinists and Dutch liberties. But he saw the expedition to the Netherlands as his guarantee of a place in the history books. Elizabeth was well aware of this, and also of the danger of entrusting too many troops to one of her subjects. So she kept a close eye on his conduct in the Netherlands. Militarily, there was little splendour in the grubby business of besieging or defending the forts and walled towns with which the country was dotted. Leicester slowed, but did not halt, Farnese's advance. He certainly lacked the resources, and probably also the skills. Politically, there were temptations aplenty, and Leicester succumbed, accepting the invitation of the Dutch to become their Governor-General in January 1586. Elizabeth was livid at what she saw as his presumptuous self-elevation to a sovereign status vying with her own. After some characteristic changes of mind, she compelled him to resign the title.

The chief concern of domestic policy through the 1580s (apart, of course, from the military and financial preparations for war) was the 'enemy within', the Roman Catholics, and above all Mary Queen of Scots, who might so easily become a focus for their discontent. The sometimes hysterical fear of Catholic plots peaked in one of the most extraordinary episodes of the reign, the making of the 'Bond of Association' in 1584, an episode which paradoxically revealed both the deep devotion of the English people to their queen and their increasing preparedness to act collectively without her lead. Inspired by the assassination of William of Orange on 10 July 1584, but conditioned by the series of plots against Elizabeth's life which were continually being uncovered, the Bond of Association was, as its title suggests, a contract or agreement of a group of people to pursue common objectives. The objectives were the protection of the queen's life and, in the event of her suspicious or sudden death, vengeance to the death against the perpetrators and beneficiaries of the deed. Modelled to some extent on the kind of political bonds and covenants which commonly figured in Scottish politics, it is a public document unique in English history for binding its signatories to commit murder under specified circumstances:

> we do not only vow and bind ourselves... never to allow, accept or favour any such pretended successors, by whom or for whom any such detestable act shall be attempted... but do also further vow and protest, as we are most bound, and that in the presence of the eternal and everliving God, to persecute such person or persons to the death with our joint and particular forces, and to take the uttermost revenge on them that by any possible means we or any of us can devise...

The subtext of the bond was the importance of keeping Mary Queen of Scots off the throne at all costs in order to defend the Protestant establishment. What is most significant about the bond is its popularity. Drafted in October by the Privy Council, and circulated by them on a county by county basis for signature by the nation's political elite, it succeeded in rapidly attracting signatures not only from most of the gentry and civic patriarchs of England, but from vast numbers of enthusiastic men of the 'middling' and 'lower' sorts. It became a nation-wide expression of loyalty. Better than anything else it symbolises the change in the religious temper of the nation since 1559. It was even signed, albeit under peer pressure, by some Catholic gentlemen here and there, and although equally some Puritan gentlemen with acute consciences held back from promising to commit murder. This explicit contract to destroy Mary Stuart simply could not have been conceived in the 1560s, when so much of the English elite remained Catholic at heart, nor promulgated in the 1570s, when hatred of 'popery' was not yet the common coin of English culture. The Bond of Association was the index not simply of a Protestant country, but of a country which would do almost anything to prevent a Catholic from taking the throne. The tone of the document was mitigated in the parliament of winter 1584-85, which reformulated the bond as an act 'for the surety of the Queen's person'. Elizabeth herself was not entirely happy with the gung-ho rough justice proposed in the original bond, and the statutory version provided for a semblance of legal process in the form of a commission of enquiry to precede any vengeance.

In the event, lynch law was not needed. Pressure for the execution of Mary Queen of Scots, which had been building up since 1570, became irresistible in the context of all-out war with Catholic Spain, especially as Philip II was now cultivating links with Mary's French relatives, the ultra-Catholic Guise dynasty. Mary sealed her own fate when she became entangled in the Babington Plot to secure her liberation and Elizabeth's assassination. Francis Walsingham, who controlled Mary's communications with the outside world, allowed her to believe that she had a secure link to a group of youthful Catholic adventurers led by the Derbyshire gentleman Anthony Babington. The whole conspiracy was so deeply penetrated by Walsingham's men, and his access to its communications so total, that apologetic claims that Mary in fact had no knowledge of the plot to kill Elizabeth are not untenable. That she was, at the least, cruelly entrapped is undeniable. Moreover, if her consent to the plot was full and informed, she might be allowed some plea of self-defence, in that the Bond of Association had put beyond any doubt the determination of the English establishment to take her life.

Once the plot was exposed, Mary was tried in a special court of English nobles. Elizabeth knew perfectly well how posterity would view any decision to execute Mary, and convened parliament in October 1586, either to consider alternatives or, more realistically, to spread the burden of guilt. Parliament added to the pressure which the Privy Council was exerting behind the scenes, and Elizabeth was impelled reluctantly, hesitantly, but inexorably, towards signing the death warrant. Even then she hesitated about executing it, and it was her Privy Council, on its own initiative, which finally despatched it. Mary was beheaded on 8 February 1587. Even Elizabeth's closest adviser, William Cecil, was in disgrace for weeks afterwards, but most of her wrath fell upon her unfortunate Secretary, William Davison, whose career was destroyed by his role in this affair. Just as Elizabeth had foreseen, the execution was used to blacken her name throughout Catholic Europe. For her enemies, it represented the crowning evil of religious persecution, and was the subject of countless pamphlets and sermons. A picture of Mary's death was made the closing image of Verstegan's *Theatre of the Cruelties of the Heretics of Our Times*, published later that year.

English intervention in the Netherlands achieved one thing. It provoked Philip II into direct action against England, partly as revenge, partly as crusade, and partly as a means of knocking England out of his Dutch problem. His decision to launch an amphibious assault against England was a fateful one. Preparations for the vast expedition occupied most of 1587, and were set back by Drake's famous raid on Cadiz. But the Armada set sail in summer 1588, and, notwithstanding persistent harrying in the English Channel from the large, experienced, superbly equipped and brilliantly led English navy, it made its way to its rendezvous off Calais. There the deficiencies of Philip II's strategy became apparent, as Farnese's invasion barges could not get out to join Medina Sidonia's deep water fleet without exposing themselves to the guns of the smaller and nimbler English and Dutch vessels. The fleet at anchor was stampeded by English fireships, and then driven away by the prevailing winds. Attempting to return home by circumnavigating the British Isles, about half the Spanish ships were sunk or wrecked by storms or enemy fire. Thousands of men were lost, dozens of ships. The English victory was total, their losses negligible.

Much of Elizabeth's reputation has been built upon her display of courage in 1588, when the landing of Spanish troops, the terror of Western Europe, seemed imminent. Her appearance at the muster of her forces at Tilbury, when she made her famous address to the troops, was an inspiring moment in the national myth. However, it was not her oratory that saved the day, but the assistance which the weather lent to her navy. Although her army, commanded by

Leicester, was large, it was fortunate not to be put to the test. The superiority of Spanish troops and tactics on land was probably as marked as the superiority of English ships and tactics at sea. But for an island power, that was the right way round, so the English victory cannot be put down solely to good fortune, however important the role of poor strategy and dire weather.

The defeat of the Armada was the high point of Elizabeth's reign. England had seen off the most powerful invasion force launched against her since the Norman Conquest, and if this was as much because of the weather as because of the strength of the nation's defences, so much the better in an age which interpreted the chances of wind and weather as the judgements of the Lord. As far as the English at the time were concerned, their victory came down to divine providence and defensive prudence. It was God's favour to England in general, and to Elizabeth in particular, which explained his providence. Victory was celebrated in verse and music, art and literature and chronicle. Elizabeth herself appeared as the saviour of her people.

There is no indication that Elizabeth herself ever had the faintest idea about what was going on in Ireland, but the 'Irish Problem' was apparent to her advisers from the start. That problem was, as the 'Device for the Alteration of Religion' pointed out, that:

> Ireland also will be very difficultly stayed in their obedience, by reason of the clergy that is so addicted to Rome.

Since the 1530s, traditional Irish Catholicism had been driven, thanks to the English Reformation, into a potent alliance with incipient Irish nationalism. Elizabeth realised, of course, that royal authority was under threat. No Tudor was slow to detect treason. But whether she could appreciate the situation in anything other than the crude polarity of obedience and rebellion is unlikely.

What was going on in Ireland was the familiar interaction of politics and religion which dominated Tudor history. But whereas the strength of personal monarchy smoothed the path of the Reformation in England, and in Wales patriotic affection for the Tudors combined with aspirations for a share in the security and spoils of the Tudor regime to the same effect, in Ireland almost everything was against the Reformation from the start, or rapidly turned out that way. English authority had never reached far beyond the Pale, and even within it the Tudor regime faced increasing problems, often because of mismanagement. While the royal supremacy was accepted relatively easily, the dissolution of the monasteries had been only partial. Irish religious orders, many of them inspired by 'observant' ideals of renewal, proved more durable than their English counterparts – although their survival was itself as much to do with the distance and ineffectiveness of royal authority as with any innate moral qualities of the Irish monks and friars.

As for the Protestant Reformation introduced under Edward VI, this never became law in Ireland. And when the zealous English Protestant John Bale was made Bishop of Ossory (an appointment which confirms that the Duke of Northumberland had a keen sense of humour), and put on one of his violently anti-Catholic plays, he was unceremoniously hounded out of town (and, when Mary came to the throne, out of the island and the queen's realms). The restoration of Catholicism under Mary, albeit a relatively simple task, relieved the Irish from only one of the irksome restraints of English rule. The attempt to use privately funded colonisation, rather than publicly funded conquest, as a cheap way of exporting English political and social culture to Ireland was actually begun in Mary's reign. The fact that the new colonies and boroughs of the 'plantations' specifically excluded native Irish people meant that the process was all too obviously being conducted at their expense rather than for their benefit.

Elizabeth's sole initial concern with Ireland was to introduce the Protestant Reformation there. But the Reformation which was carried through the Dublin parliament early in 1560 by the Earl of Sussex, Lord Deputy of Ireland, was being sown on untilled ground, and found it hard to put down roots. Much of Ireland was entirely outside English control, though none of it out of reach of English punitive expeditions. Ireland was a perpetual drain on English resources. Elizabeth was never prepared to put in the kind of money which might have sufficed to introduce the English model of government to which English policy aspired. It is doubtful anyway whether England actually had the resources which would have been needed for the job. The aims of policy were variously to prevent and suppress rebellion, and to keep out or expel foreign powers. The overriding priority was to prevent Ireland from becoming a threat to England. At times, notably in the 1590s, even this modest objective required funding on a huge scale.

As Anglo-Spanish relations deteriorated in the 1570s, Philip II looked to foment unrest in Elizabeth's backyard. It was a small force of Spanish and Italian mercenaries which sparked off the rebellion of the Fitzgeralds of Munster in 1579. The rebellion was largely defeated within a year, but the English troops ravaged the province for years before capturing and killing the head of the Fitzgeralds, the Earl of Desmond, in 1583. When, in the 1590s, weak government by successive Lord Deputies fuelled the ambition of the Earl of Tyrone and he launched a rebellion, Philip II was once more ready to assist. The English government was cornered into seeking the military reduction of the entire island. This reluctant conquest was eventually achieved early in 1603, thanks to the efforts of Elizabeth's last Lord Deputy, Charles Blount, Lord Mountjoy. Elizabeth's problems with Ireland were at an end, but English problems with Ireland were barely beginning.

IX

THE EARL OF ESSEX: 1589-1601

English politics in the 1590s was dominated by the figure of the queen's new favourite, Robert Devereux, Earl of Essex. William Cecil remained her chief minister until his death in 1598, and his son Robert Cecil, groomed for succession by his father and recruited to the Privy Council as Secretary in 1591, imperceptibly took over the reins. Yet it was Essex who bestrode the scene, though he proved a meteoric rather than a colossal figure. Succeeding in effect to the place vacated in 1588 by the death of Leicester, his stepfather and patron (having already succeeded him as Master of the Horse in 1587), Essex was the more talented and ambitious of the two, but also arguably the less stable. Like Leicester, he yearned for military glory: indeed, he was said to be 'entirely given over to arms and war'. Unlike Leicester, he was to be given a serious chance of winning it. Forbidden by the queen from joining the naval expedition against Lisbon, he went anyway, and was summoned back in short-lived disgrace. Denied leadership of an expedition to France in 1589, he was awarded his first command on another such expedition in 1592 – without notable success. His return at least saw him promoted to the Privy Council, but military ambition was once more fanned by the opportunity of leading another seaborne assault against Philip II, this time a raid on Cadiz, in 1596.

Essex's raid was in itself something of a success. Cadiz was sacked, and it was not his fault that he was not able to add a Spanish treasure fleet to the plunder. Yet this time his return exposed the gulf between masculine and feminine estimates of military glory. Loot was of more interest to Elizabeth than honour in battle, and hardly any was brought back. For her, the expedition was simply another loss-making venture. From this time, his relations with the queen began to deteriorate. Elizabeth grew doubtful about his pride, ambition and jealousy, while Essex saw the relentless rise of Robert Cecil in the Privy Council as a threat to his own position. Leicester had accepted the primacy of the father, but Essex resented the successes of the son. The conflict between the 'sword', the old concept of the nobility as based in military service to the Crown, and the 'pen', the new concept of service in administration (which in France came to be called the 'robe'), was exemplified in their rivalry. Another voyage against the Spanish in 1597 brought Essex no change in his fortunes, as it once more failed to intercept the treasure fleet. His temper was not improved by discovering, on his return, that Robert Cecil had secured the profitable post of Chancellor of the Duchy of Lancaster. Elizabeth managed to coax him out of his despondency by bestowing upon him the office of Earl Marshal, one of the very highest titles at her disposal.

It was Ireland which led to Essex's undoing, as to that of many other English politicians. First, his underlying weaknesses reappeared in a quarrel between him and the Cecils during 1598 over who should be the new Lord Deputy of Ireland. In a personal interview with Essex, Elizabeth made it plain that she was taking the Cecils' advice. Furious, Essex turned his back on her – a mortal insult to her royal status.

She slapped him, and he reached for his sword. Although bystanders prevented this ugly scene from going any further, Essex stormed out, proclaiming that not even from Henry VIII himself would he have accepted such treatment. He was wrong, of course. Nobody had ever tried anything like that in front of Henry VIII, and to have done so would have meant certain and rapid death.

As affairs in Ireland went from bad to worse, Elizabeth's government was faced with the necessity of despatching overwhelming force to suppress the rebellion there. This time, there was no quarrel about whom to put in charge. Essex was the only credible choice, and the offer was one that, for all his misgivings, he simply could not refuse. He had always wanted a major command, though he had wanted it in the glamorous European theatre, not among the bogs and woods of the 'other island'. Crossing to Dublin in April 1599 with the largest army ever sent to Tudor Ireland, he rapidly showed that he was no Farnese. He did not know what to do, and he did not know how to hold his army together. His position weakening, he ignored his clear instructions to attack the Earl of Tyrone and in September opened unauthorised negotiations which resulted in a truce. Without permission to abandon his command he then hurried home to justify his actions. Elizabeth was prepared to condone neither his disobedience nor his failure. He was put under house arrest, stripped of his offices, and rusticated. His incompetence was thrown into relief by the achievement of his successor, Lord Mountjoy, who, over the next couple of years, with inferior resources to those lavished upon Essex, methodically crushed the rebels, destroyed a substantial expeditionary force sent from Spain, and secured Tyrone's surrender.

Essex, however, would not accept his fate. Putting together a motley array of disaffected soldiers, ambitious and under funded younger sons, and even some hopeful Catholics, as well as one or two more substantial but still marginal figures, he sought to launch a coup in February 1601. If he could not win the queen's favour, he proposed to extort it. The coup as it unfolded can seem almost mindless in retrospect. Starting from his town house in the Strand with barely 200 men, he headed into London with a view to raising popular support for a march on the Court complex. It is hard to see how he hoped to succeed.

The answer probably lies in the recent example of another disaffected but popular military hero (and although Elizabeth and her Council had now seen through Essex's pretensions, the aura of the popular military hero still hung about him). The Duke of Guise had seized power in Paris back in 1585 in much this fashion, as the Paris mobs rallied to his cause and swelled the few hundred men with which he had started his march upon the French Court. But if Essex had read his modern history, he had not read closely enough. Guise had launched his coup against a massively unpopular monarch in a city where his network of support was dense in the context of intermittent but bitter civil wars fuelled by religious hatred. Essex, in contrast, overplayed a weak hand. His was a falling star and Elizabeth still commanded enormous popular loyalty. Londoners were bemused but unmoved by Essex's appeals, and he gave himself up. Briskly tried for treason, he was beheaded on 25 February.

Although the instability of her last favourite was the political problem which confronted Elizabeth most personally in the 1590s, it was far from the most serious. Naval war with Spain, intervention in France on behalf of Henry IV (whose claim to the throne was contested by the militant Catholic faction there, with Spanish backing), and the repression of rebellion in Ireland placed intolerable financial strains upon her regime. These were intensified by years of poor harvests, and by their inevitable accompaniment: epidemic disease.

Demographically, the disasters of the 1590s were second only to those of the 1550s in the Tudor era. Economically, things may even have been worse, although her councillors remembered the lessons of the 1540s and 1550s, and at least resisted the last temptation of debasing the currency. Partly because of that self-denial, the financial position of the Crown had never been worse. Long-term inflation had reduced the real value of customs duties and, together with almost systematic under-assessment of the wealth of the nobility and gentry, had massively eroded the real yields of direct taxation. The one novel financial expedient of the period, selling or issuing trade monopolies, not only compounded economic dislocation but for a while soured Elizabeth's relations with her parliament. The domestic strains of foreign war and economic crisis in turn undermined law and order, and the Privy Council was having to meet on a daily basis to cope.

All this, added to the uncertainty over the succession, might have amounted to a crisis every bit as bad as that of 1558. Yet the severity of the problems serves chiefly to highlight the extraordinary success of Elizabeth and her government in defending and governing the country through these difficult years. There was neither a baronial nor a popular revolt. Essex's attempted coup in 1601 made him look ridiculous. What held the country together was a combination of nationalism, Protestantism, and loyalism, focused on the person, or perhaps on the image, of Elizabeth herself.

The image of Elizabeth which did so much to hold the country together through the crisis of the 1590s was built upon the foundations of monarchical ideology which had been laid by her predecessors, notably Henry VII and in particular Henry VIII. The general Tudor myth of the monarch as the sole bulwark against anarchy was given particular expression in the person of Elizabeth. Moreover, it was an image which was built up gradually and deliberately through the reign. Elizabeth herself was always concerned with the public face of her words and actions, and she chose and designed them carefully in order to put across favourable impressions of herself; hence her care to distance herself as far as possible from unpleasant or unpopular proceedings. It was the bishops who had to suppress unwanted manifestations of Puritanism. It was her councillors and servants who had to bear the brunt of responsibility for executing Mary Queen of Scots. It would be going too far to see her as a practitioner of 'spin' along the lines of modern political media manipulation. But she showed something of the same concern with her image.

There was positive image-making as well as a shrewd management of the negative. The progresses which presented the queen to her subjects, although confined within the English heartlands of the south and east, were filled with civic receptions and public entertainments which put across positive images of Elizabeth as a Protestant paragon, a dispenser of justice, a bringer of peace and a defender of the realm. Themes such as these ran through the splendid entertainment laid on by the Earl of Leicester at his great castle of Kenilworth for a royal visit in 1575. With fireworks and water features, music and pageants, this was one of the most spectacular shows of the Tudor era. It took months to prepare, and was recorded for posterity in a pamphlet written by one of Leicester's clients. Official propaganda was by no means unknown, but alongside it there was a barrage of printed material produced by well-wishers of various kinds: hack writers in search of reward, clergy out for preferment, minor officials in search of promotion and public office. And in between the official propaganda and the private enterprise variety was a host of further publications, many of them hugely influential, which struck the same notes. John Foxe's 'Book of Martyrs', the *Acts and Monuments*, issued in successive and expanding editions, may have been international in its scope and intention, but its readers drew from it a national myth in which Elizabeth – presented by Foxe as a woman denied her martyr's crown only by a special and greater providence of God – played a decisive role.

Elizabeth's Court, too, played its part in presenting a glorious picture of the queen to her people. From the ordinary offices of its daily life and the regular ceremonies of the Chapel Royal to the set-pieces of Accession Day celebrations and tournaments (which emerged in the 1570s) and grand State processions, there was usually something to impress the visitor to London and Westminster. Audiences for such displays might consist largely of Londoners, foreign dignitaries and visiting country gentry – but it was a socially, and perhaps also a statistically, significant fraction of the population which at some time or other saw the queen in her splendour. The portraiture and poetry in which the creation of the queen's image is seen at its most sophisticated, most of which was produced and circulated within the context of the Court, was inevitably accessible and comprehensible only to a restricted audience. But simpler messages about the queen were widely disseminated.

Parliament gave the queen and her councillors a national stage on which to perform. Although, in accordance with its role, parliament served as a sounding-board for the grievances of the people (especially those of the gentry and civic leaders who populated the House of Commons), the long historiographical tradition which has seen parliament as a forum for growing 'opposition' to the Crown in Elizabeth's reign has fundamentally mistaken the nature and purpose of the institution at that time. It was there to vote taxation, to help enact legislation, and to offer advice to the Crown. Elizabeth got the laws she wanted and got tax, although often not as much as she wanted. She tended perhaps to get rather more advice than she wanted, which was where most of the tensions arose between her and the House of Commons. But few members of her parliaments would have wished to classify themselves as 'opposition' in the sense in which the term is used today. To oppose the monarch was to be at best a disobedient subject, at worst a traitor or a rebel. The Catholic bishops opposed the religious settlement in 1559 – and all but one were subsequently deprived of their bishoprics. Most of the trouble Elizabeth had with her parliaments was over unwelcome advice: on further religious change, on the succession, on Mary Queen of Scots, on foreign policy, on how to deal with Catholics. Often enough, troublesome MPs were mouthpieces or stalking-horses for Elizabeth's own Privy Councillors, using parliament as an extra forum for urging their policies upon the queen. As a woman she inevitably suffered, in a way that a competent king usually would not, from the casual assumption by the men of her Council and indeed of her parliaments that they knew more of the ways of the world than she did.

Despite her imperious way with unwanted advice, Elizabeth knew how to charm her parliaments. Her responses to delegations from the Commons were carefully scripted and widely reported. In Lords and Commons, her councillors were tireless in putting over the themes of peace, Protestantism and prosperity as the fruits of her rule. And when grievances became acute, as in the intense agitation against monopolies around 1600, she knew how to make concessions graciously and to maximum effect. Parliament was, in short, an important 'point of contact' between Crown and country.

Above all, the daily and weekly liturgical offices of the Church of England drummed home a message of obedience and loyalty, from the daily prayers for the queen to special services of thanksgiving for her accession or for deliverance from dangers. With the 'Homily against Disobedience and Wilful Rebellion' regularly read in parish churches across the land, the duties of the subject were constantly reiterated:

As in reading of the holy Scriptures we shall find in very many and almost infinite places, as well of the Old Testament as of the New, that kings and princes, as well the evil as the good, do reign by God's ordinance, and that subjects are bounden to obey them... such subjects as are disobedient or rebellious against their princes, disobey God and procure their own damnation...

...all kings, queens, princes, and other governors are specially appointed by the ordinance of God.

And with the royal coat of arms prominently displayed in those churches, where paintings of the crucifixion or the Last Judgement had once had their place, the sacred status of the crown was unmistakably proclaimed to everyone.

Elizabeth worked at her contemporary image in ways in which previous monarchs had worked at their memory. The media, the Court, parliament and the Church all played their part in creating that image, which had a more lasting impact on posterity than the memorials on which other monarchs spent so heavily. Her reign was a great age for building, and saw some of the greatest houses in the land go up: for example, Hardwick Hall and Burghley House. It was also a great age for foundations: grammar schools and almshouses were established in towns across the country, and one or two colleges in Oxford and Cambridge. Yet Elizabeth, unlike her four Tudor predecessors, built and founded nothing (with the partial exception of the collegiate church at what we still call Westminster Abbey, which she 'founded' at no real cost to herself after she had closed down the actual monastery). Of their palaces and colleges and hospitals and religious houses, some have survived and some have fallen. But her portraiture and literature have, ultimately, proved more durable than their architecture.

X

DEATH: 1603

Elizabeth died at Richmond in the early hours of 24 March 1603. A London diarist with a friend at Court reported her death in the following words:

> This morning, about three o'clock, Her Majesty departed this life, mildly like a lamb, easily like a ripe apple from the tree, *cum leve quadam febre, absque gemitu* [with a slight shiver, without a groan]. Dr Parry told me that he was present, and sent his prayers before her soul. I doubt not but she is amongst the royal saints in Heaven in eternal joys.

It was not all as serene as the publicity implied. Despite her great age – only a small minority saw their seventieth year in those days – and despite having undergone severe illnesses at several points, Elizabeth was not reconciled to dying. What proved to be her final illness set in late in 1602 and thereafter her decline was steady. Even her mind began to weaken, though not to the extent that she allowed the physicians to hasten her end with their quack remedies. Unable to eat much, unwilling to sleep, her last days were difficult. Today we would say that she had a strong will to live. Tudor England was more intimate with death, in all its forms, and the classical and medieval notion of the 'good death' was still widely held. Yet neither Elizabeth's religion nor perhaps her preferred stoic philosophy provided her with consolation in her last days. Nor were there the social consolations of friends and family. She had outlived friends and favourites, contemporaries and juniors. Leicester had died in 1588; Cecil, infirm and increasingly deaf, in 1598; and she had signed Essex's death-warrant just two years before. It is said that she was hit particularly hard by the death in February 1603 of her old friend and cousin Katherine Carey, Countess of Nottingham (wife of Lord Howard of Effingham, and a companion of hers since the start of her reign). Elizabeth's reluctance to face death was of a piece with that reluctance to face the inevitable which she had often shown in her royal career. It is symbolised in her failure to make a will.

Reports from her deathbed vary hugely in their details. According to one, she asked Whitgift to pray for her. According to the recollections of one of her ladies in waiting, Lady Southwell, she sent him packing with the comment that he and his kind were nothing but 'hedge-priests'. Lady Southwell's testimony betrays her own Catholic inclinations, and may therefore be suspect at least of embroidery in its desire to tell a good story against the Church of England. On the other hand, the words she puts on Elizabeth's lips seem to carry the familiar lash of the royal tongue. This same report includes another story which bears all the hallmarks of authenticity. The succession to the throne had by now been wrapped up by Robert Cecil's secret diplomacy with James VI of Scotland, who was soon to become James I of England. Yet even now her hopeful councillors sought some kind of answer from her on this, the oldest unanswered question of her reign. Believing her unable to speak, they offered to run through a list of candidates and asked her to lift a finger if she wished to approve one. Various names, including that of the King of Scots, left her unmoved. But at the name of Lord Beauchamp, a male descendant of the Grey line, she burst into life: 'I will have no rascal's son in my seat, but one worthy to be a king'. Yet she literally would not lift a finger to solve the problem. Hesitating to the end, she lost consciousness a little later in the day, and died in the night.

The mortal Moon hath her eclipse endured...
(Shakespeare, Sonnet CVII)

FURTHER READING

The story of Elizabeth Tudor told here makes no claims to the status of 'original research'. Its information is for the most part the 'common knowledge' of history and biography, and it would be redundant to attempt to document it with the formal apparatus of footnotes and bibliography. The interpretation is my own to the extent that the combination of the judgements here passed upon her character and policy is personal, though few if any of the judgements will not have been anticipated somewhere in the vast literature upon her. The following selection from the scholarly literature which has helped form my own interpretation of Elizabeth is offered as a starting-point and guide for those who wish to form their own interpretation in their turn.

Biographies of Elizabeth are thick on the shelves, and there is sadly little to choose between most of them. But Wallace MacCaffrey's *Elizabeth I* (Arnold, 1993),focusing more on political than personal issues, is the judgement of a scholar whose life's work has been devoted to the exploration of the politics of the reign in a series of influential monographs. And David Starkey's *Elizabeth: Apprenticeship* (Chatto & Windus, 2000), which wears its learning lightly and addresses a wide readership with a sparkling style, offers some genuinely new insights into the political formation of the last Tudor monarch, giving a sense of what might be done for Elizabeth's whole life if the story was rewritten from the ground up. Carole Levin's *The Heart and Stomach of a King: Elizabeth I and the Politics of Sex and Power* (University of Pennsylvania Press, 1994) is a stimulating reflection on how Elizabeth coped with the problem of being a female ruler in a man's world. Christopher Haigh's thematic study, *Elizabeth I* (new edn, Longman, 2001) is a *tour de force*, persuasively and wittily written, and packed with acute analysis of the queen and of the politics of her reign. G.R. Elton's *The Parliament of England, 1559–1581* (CUP, 1986) entirely and convincingly rewrote this hitherto badly misunderstood passage of English history.

The lives of Leicester, Essex, and other leading men of Elizabeth's Court have been endlessly retold, in biographies often as undistinguished and indistinguishable as those of their sovereign. However, Paul Hammer's *The Polarisation of Elizabethan Politics* (CUP, 1999), the first instalment of a comprehensive account of Robert Devereux, Earl of Essex, taking the story to 1597, is a penetrating insight into both the world of the new nobility created by the Tudors and the later politics of the reign. There is a great deal in the two studies by Conyers Read, *Mr Secretary Cecil and Queen Elizabeth* and *Lord Burghley and Queen Elizabeth* (Jonathan Cape, 1955 and 1960), but William Cecil awaits a definitive biography. In the meantime, M.A.R. Graves, *Burghley* (Longman, 1998) is a useful students' introduction, while Stephen Alford's *The Early Elizabethan Polity: William Cecil and the British Succession Crisis, 1558–1569* (CUP, 1998) shows what can be done, giving a profound and persuasive analysis of Cecil's policy. Elizabeth's bishops have not recently attracted anything like the interest shown in their predecessors, with the shining exception of Patrick Collinson's *Archbishop Grindal, 1519–1583* (Jonathan Cape, 1979). Collinson's article 'The Monarchical Republic of Queen Elizabeth I', which appeared in the *Bulletin of the John Rylands Library*, 69 (1987), pp.394–424, opened an entirely new window on the politics of Elizabethan England. The war with Spain, and in particular the Armada campaign, has a vast literature. Colin Martin and Geoffrey Parker, *The Spanish Armada* (Hamish Hamilton, 1988) is the best place to start. Important aspects of the 'myth' of Elizabeth are explored in Frances Yates, *Astraea* (Routledge & Kegan Paul, 1975) and Roy Strong, *The Cult of Elizabeth* (Thames and Hudson, 1977).

LIST OF ILLUSTRATIONS

TA pictures courtesy of the Tempus Archive
JR pictures courtesy of Jonathan Reeve

1. Archbishop Warham by Hans Holbein.
    TA CD 12 37
2. Thomas Cranmer by Gerlach Flicke. TA CD 5
    18.
3. Executions for treason at Tyburn. TA CD 20 121
    15001550.
4. Henry VIII by Hans Holbein. TA CD 12 25c.
5. John Bale. TA 502 15501600.
6. The burning of Anne Askewe. TA CD 20 33
    15001550.
7. Prayers written out by Princess Elizabeth.
    JR 221b5fp286 15501600.

8.   Edward, Prince of Wales, the future Edward
     VI. TA CD 12 30.

9.   Jane Seymour by Hans Holbein. TA CD 12 28.

10. William Cecil, Lord Burghley. TA505
     15501600.

11. Lady Jane Grey. TA503 15501600.

12. The burning of John Rogers. TA CD 20 139
     15501600.

13. Philip II of Spain. JR188b4p823 15501600.

14. London Bridge. JR CD 3 997.

15. Portrait engraving of Mary, Queen of
     England. TA CD 14 57.

16. The execution of Thomas Cranmer. TA CD 20
     141.

17. The Tower of London. JR CD 3 1025.

18. Great Seal of Elizabeth I. TA CD 11 442.

19. St Paul's Church. TA CD 20 177.

20. Robert Dudley by F. Hogenberg. JR203b5fp4
     15501600.

21. Edwin Sandys. TA504 15501600.

22. Plan of the palaces of Westminster and
     Whitehall. JR CD 3 769.

23. The Entrance of Queen Elizabeth. JR201b5p2
     15501600.

24. Preaching at Paul's Cross, London. JR209b5p68
     15501600.

25. Alexander Nowell, Dean of St Paul's. TA507
     15501600.

26. Edmund Bonner, Bishop of London.

JR239b7p321 15501600.

27. The *Book of Common Prayer*, 1559. JR CD 3 1021.

28. Title-page of the first Marprelate Tract. JRCD 3 1029.

29. John Knox. JR125b2p535 15501600.

30. Elizabeth I enjoying a picnic. JR173b4p741 15501600.

31. Elizabeth I and her huntsman. JR125b2p535 15501600

32. Elizabeth I hawking. JR172b4p740 15501600.

33. Chess and draughts. JR160b3p477 15501600.

34. George Gascoigne presenting a book to Queen Elizabeth. JR143b3fp186 15501600.

35. Parsons and Campion. JR207b5p50 15501600.

36. Queen Elizabeth at the opening of parliament. TA CD 20 79 15501600.

37. The Red Cross Knight from Edmund Spenser's *The Faerie Queen*. JR194b4p856 15501600.

38. Mary Queen of Scots. TA CD 8 21c.

39. Letter from Mary Queen of Scots to Elizabeth. JR240b7p392 15501600.

40. The Royal Exchange. JR182b4p787 15501600.

41. Roman Catholic plots against Elizabeth. JR129b2p601 15501600.

42. Title-page of the 'Thirty-Nine Articles', 1571. JRCD 3 1028.

43. Acts of Parliament, 1585. JR187b4p811

15501600.

44. Francis Walsingham. TA506 15501600.

45. The Spanish Armada off the French coast. JR216b5p148 15501600.

46. Fernando Alvárez de Toledo, Duke of Alva. JR189b4p824 15501600.

47. 'A Hieroglyphic of Britain'. JR174b4p743 15501600.

48. Sir Francis Drake. JR191b4p830 15501600.

49. Nonsuch House. TA CD 20 89 15501600.

50. William of Orange. JR190b4p827 15501600.

51. Anthony Babington and his conspirators. JR204b5p9 15501600.

52. The arrangement of the hall of Fotheringay Castle for the trial of Mary Queen of Scots in October 1586. JR241b7p397 15501600.

53. Title page of a thanksgiving service issued in 1588. JR242b7p405 15501600.

54. English troops on the march in Ireland. JR214b5fp138 15501600.

55. The reception of Sir Henry Sidney by the mayor and aldermen of Dublin. JR197b4p921t 15501600.

56. Engraved portrait of Elizabeth I. JR171b4p734 15501600.

57. Hugh O'Neill, Earl of Tyrone. JR213b5p116 15501600.

58. Francis Bacon. JR226b5fp406 15501600.

59. Portrait of Queen Elizabeth. TA CD 14 68.

60. Sir Edward Coke. JR235b6p195 15501600.
61. Outdoor entertainments at Elvetham. JR211b5p104 15501600.
62. Richard Tarlton. JR149b3fp258 15501600.
63. 'The Procession Picture'. JR200b5pii 15501600.
64. State barge and water procession. JR232b6p76 15501600.
65. The Bear Garden and the Globe Theatre. TA CD 20, 342 15501600.

INDEX

Alva, Duke of, Fernando
    Alvarez de Toledo fig. 46,
    175, 177
Anne Boleyn, Queen 13-14,
    16-17, 19, 20, 21, 37, 52,
    56, 60, 103
Anne of Cleves 26
Armada, Spanish fig. 45, fig.
    53, 172, 192-93
Arthur, Prince of Wales (d
    1502) 15
Ascham, Roger 24-25, 64, 76
Ashley, Katherine 29, 45,
    89-90
  assassination 110, 170-71,
    184, 187-88, 190

Babington Plot 190
Bacon, Francis, Viscount St
    Albans (d. 1626) fig. 58
Bacon, Nicholas, knight 56

Bale, John fig. 5, 195
Barton, Elizabeth, 'Holy Maid
    of Kent' 20
Bedingfield, Henry, knight
    44-45
Bible 15, 44, 60, 61, 62, 78,
    79, 211
bishops 71-74, 75, 78, 85, 92,
    93, 99, 206, 209
Blount, Charles, Lord
    Mountjoy (d. 1606) 197,
    203
Bond of Association 187-89,
    190
Bonner, Edmund, Bishop of
    London (d. 1569) 72,
    fig. 26
Bowes, Sir George 10
Bromley, Thomas, knight 56

Cadiz 192, 200

Calais 46, 53, 82, 86-87, 192

Calvin, John 67, 79, 80

Cambridge 24, 25, 32, 50, 56, 212

Campion, Edmund 119, fig. 35

Catherine of Aragon 14, 20, 22, 24, 37, 46, 52, 54, 61

Catherine Parr, Queen 23, 26, 27-29, 103

Catholicism, Roman 37-38, 65, 68, 72-73, 117-20, 169-72

Cecil, William, Lord Burghley (d. 1598) 32-33, 47, 50, 55-56, 58, 64, 70, 80, 82-86, 87-88, 96, 97, 114, 115, 119, fig. 10, fig. 53, 169, 172, 174, 190, 199, 214

Cecil, Robert, Earl of Salisbury (d. 1612) 199, 201, 215

Chapuys, Eustace, imperial ambassador 14, 17, 21

Charles V, Holy Roman Emperor and King of Spain 14, 15, 40, 41

Common Prayer, Books of 30, 64, fig. 27

Convocation 71-72

Council, Privy 30, 31, 41, 43, 44, 45, 49, 50, 55-56, 77, 84, 100, 105, 113, 180-82, 188, 191, 199, 200, 201, 203, 205, 209-10

Court, royal 20, 22, 27, 37, 45, 49, 51, 88-90, 100, 102, fig. 34, 175, 181, 208, 212, 213

Courtenay, Edward, Earl of Devon (d. 1556) 39, 41-42

Cranmer, Thomas Archbishop of Canterbury (d. 1556) 16, 17, 21, 30, fig. 2, fig. 16

Devereux, Robert, Earl of Essex (d. 1601) 57-58, 181, 199-204, 205-206, 214

Dormer, Jane, Lady 32, 38, 49

Drake, Francis, knight fig. 48, 184, 192

Dublin fig. 55, 196, 202

Dudley, John, Duke of Northumberland (d. 1553) 31, 33, 35-37, 195

Dudley, Robert, Earl of Leicester (d. 1588) 57-58, 64, 87, 90, 94, 97, 99, 101, 102, 103, 112, fig. 20, 181, 185-87, 199-200, 201, 207, 214

Durham 9, 11, 65, 117

East Anglia 31, 36

Edward VI 22, 23, 27, 29, 31-32, 35, 49, 59, 60, 81, fig. 8, 195

Eltham 20

Elizabeth I
  accession 49-50, 52, 55, fig. 23, 208
  bastard 21-22, 27, 36, 37, 52, 60, 62, 94, 101
  birth 13-14, 17
  caution 83, 112-13
  christening 17

coronation 51
courage 43, 192
death 213–16
education 23–25, 64, 76–77
excommunicated by pope
117
favourites 57–58
marriage prospects 25–26,
28, 29, 39, 54, 95–97,
102–103, 178–82
mercy 8, 11, 170
piety 38, 44–45, 51, 60–70,
fig. 7, 215
views on marriage 95–99,
102–105
virginity 90, 96, 100–101
Enfield 27
eucharist/mass 11, 30, 32,
37–38, 49, 64, 65–66, 68,
73, 85
executions 8–10, 20, 38, 43,
64, 66, 68, 116–17, 119,
120, fig. 3, fig. 6, fig. 12,
fig. 17, 177, 190–91, 204,
206

Farnese, Alessandro, Duke of
Parma and Piacenza 179,
185, 192, 202
Fetherstone, Richard 23, 64
Fisher, John, Bishop of
Rochester (d. 1535) 24
Fortescue, John, knight 56
Foxe, John 61, 119, 120, 207–
208
France 46, 54, 55, 83, 85,
86–87, 108, 176–77, 184,
185, 201
Francis I, King of France 16,
63

Francis II, King of France 53,
81–82, 85, 108
Francis, de Valois, Duke of
Anjou 90, 97, 178–82

Gardiner, Stephen, Bishop of
Winchester (d. 1555) 39,
41–42, 43, 59
Greenwich 17, 21, 26
Grindal, Edmund, Archbishop
of Canterbury (d. 1583)
65, 66, 78

Hampton Court 22, 45, 86
Hatfield 19, 22, 33, 36, 45, 50
Hatton, Christopher, knight
57–58, 181
Henry IV, King of France 67,
171, 204
Henry VIII 9, 13–17, 20–22,
24, 26, 31, 36, 41, 46, 49,
52, 53, 54, 60, 61, 62, 63,
80, 81, 93–94, 109, 116,
fig. 4, 186, 202, 206
Hertford 22, 27
Howard, Charles, 2nd Baron
Howard of Effingham, 1st
Earl of Nottingham (d.
1624) 56, 214
Howard, Thomas, 3rd Duke
of Norfolk (d. 1554) 17
Howard, Thomas, 4th Duke
of Norfolk (d. 1572) 98,
101, 114–17, 118

Ireland 88, fig. 54, 184, 193–
97, 201–203

James VI and I, King of

Scotland and England 60,
109, 215
Jane Grey, Lady 36, 38, fig. 11
Jane Seymour, Queen 21, 22,
31, fig. 9

Kenilworth 207
Kent 39
Knollys, Francis, knight 55
Knox, John 79–80, 82, 85,
fig. 29

London 17, 20, 37, 39–40, 43,
50, 73, 203–204, 208
St Paul's Cathedral fig. 19
Tower of London 21, 30,
42–43, 64, 91, 117, fig. 17

Mary I 9, 14, 17, 19, 21–22,
26–27, 31–32, 35–41, 42,
44, 45–47, 49, 50, 51, 52,
53, 55, 57, 63, 71, 72, 79,
86–87, 93, 102–103, 104,
110, 112, 113, fig. 15,
170, 195
Mary, Queen of Scots 46, 53,
81–82, 85, 98, 101, 103,
107–15, 117, 118, fig. 38,
fig. 39, fig. 53, 175, 177,
179, 184, 187–90, 206,
209
More, Thomas, knight 22, 24,
69, 185
music 69–70

navy 192–93
Netherlands 79, 173–76, 177,
178–79, 185, 191
Nowell, Alexander fig. 25

Oxford 212

Parker, Matthew, Archbishop
of Canterbury (d. 1575)
64, 76, 96
parliament 70–71, 72, 73, 75,
91–93, 104–105, 113, 118,
120, fig. 36, fig. 42, 169,
179, 190, 208–209, 212
Act of Succession (1534)
19–20, 52, 64
Act of Succession (1536)
21, 52
Act of Succession (1544)
27, 36–37, 52, 109
Act of Supremacy (1559)
74
Act of Uniformity (1559)
74
Act for the Surety of the
Queen's Person (1585)
189
Parry, Thomas, knight 29, 32,
55, 56
Philip II, King of England and
Spain (d. 1598) 38–39, 41,
46, 50, 53, 54–55, 103, fig.
13, 173, 175–76, 179, 183,
190, 191–92, 196–97, 200
Pius V, Pope 117
Portugal 183–84, 200
preaching 65, 66, 67, 84,
fig. 24, 210–11
Puritans 66, 67, 69, 76–79,
169, 206

Radcliffe, Thomas, Earl of
Sussex (d. 1583) 9, 42,
101, 116, 180, 196
Raleigh, Walter, knight 57–58,

181

rebellion 31, 33, 39, 115–17, 175, 177, 180, 197, 210–11

Reformation, Protestant 35

Renard, Simon, imperial ambassador 40–41, 42

royal supremacy 13, 64, 74, 84

Sackville, Richard, knight 55

Sandys, Edwin, Archbishop of York (d. 1588) fig. 21

Scotland 79, 81 86, 87, 108, 110–11, 184, 188

Seymour, Edward, Duke of Somerset (d. 1551) 27–31, 32

Seymour, Thomas, Lord Sudeley (d. 1549) 27–30, 33, 97

Spain 174–76, 178, 203

war with 172, 183–87, 191–93, 196–97, 200–201, 204

Stokesley, John, Bishop of London (d. 1538) 17

Thirty-Nine Articles 118, fig. 41

Throckmorton, Nicholas, knight 54

treason 29, 112, 118, 119, fig. 40, fig. 51, 184, 187, 189, 203,

Vavasour, Ann 58

Vere, Edward de, 17th Earl of Oxford (d. 1604) 58

Vives, Juan Luis 23

Walsingham, Francis, knight 99, fig. 43, 169, 171, 184, 189

Warham, William, Archbishop of Canterbury (d. 1532) 16, fig. 1

Westminster Abbey 51, 72, 212

Whitehall 40, 42, 91, fig. 22

Whitgift, John, Archbishop of Canterbury (d. 1604) 77–78, 215

Wyatt, Thomas, knight 38 40, 41, 43, 46

Yorkshire 10

TEMPUS – REVEALING HISTORY

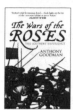

The Wars of the Roses
The Soldiers' Experience
ANTHONY GOODMAN
'A fascinating book' *TLS*
£12.99
0 7524 3731 3

The Vikings
MAGNUS MAGUNSSON
'Serious, engaging history'
BBC History Magazine
£9.99
0 7524 2699 0

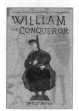

William the Conqueror
DAVID BATES
'As expertly woven as the Bayeux Tapestry'
BBC History Magazine
£12.99
0 7524 2960 4

Agincourt: A New History
ANNE CURRY
'A tour de force' *Alison Weir*
'*The* book on the battle' *Richard Holmes*
A BBC History Magazine BOOK OF THE YEAR 2005
£12.99
0 7524 2828 4

Hereward The Last Englishman
PETER REX
'An enthralling work of historical detection'
Robert Lacey
£17.99
0 7524 3318 0

The English Resistance
The Underground War Against the Normans
PETER REX
'An invaluable rehabilitation of an ignored
resistance movement' *The Sunday Times*
£12.99
0 7524 3733 X

Richard III
MICHAEL HICKS
'A most important book by the greatest living
expert on Richard' *Desmond Seward*
£9.99
0 7524 2589 7

The Peasants' Revolt
England's Failed Revolution of 1381
ALASTAIR DUNN
'A stunningly good book... totally absorbing'
Melvyn Bragg
£9.99
0 7524 2965 5

If you are interested in purchasing other books published by Tempus, or in case you have difficulty finding
any Tempus books in your local bookshop, you can also place orders directly through our website:
www.tempus-publishing.com

TEMPUS – REVEALING HISTORY

William II Rufus, the Red King
EMMA MASON
'A thoroughly new reappraisal of a much
maligned king. The dramatic story of his life is
told with great pace and insight'
John Gillingham

£25

0 7524 3528 0

William Wallace The True Story of Braveheart
CHRIS BROWN
'A formidable new biography... sieves through
masses of medieval records to distinguish the
man from the myth' *Magnus Magnusson*

£17.99

0 7524 3432 2

Elizabeth Wydeville: The Slandered Queen
ARLENE OKERLUND
'A penetrating, thorough and wholly
convincing vindication of this unlucky queen'
Sarah Gristwood
'A gripping tale of lust, loss and tragedy'
Alison Weir
A *BBC History Magazine* Book of the Year 2005

£9.99   978 07524 3807 8

The Battle of Hastings 1066
M.K. LAWSON
'Blows away many fundamental assumptions
about the battle of Hastings... an exciting and
indispensable read' *David Bates*
A *BBC History Magazine* Book of the Year 2003

£12.99   978 07524 4177 1

The Welsh Wars of Independence
DAVID MOORE
'Beautifully written, subtle and remarkably
perceptive' *John Davies*

£12.99

978 07524 4128 3

Medieval England
From Hastings to Bosworth
EDMUND KING
'The best illustrated history of medieval
England' *John Gillingham*

£12.99

0 7524 2827 5

A Companion to Medieval England
NIGEL SAUL
'Wonderful... everything you could wish to
know about life in medieval England'
Heritage Today

£19.99

0 7524 2969 8

The Prince In The Tower
MICHAEL HICKS
'The first time in ages that a publisher has sent
me a book I actually want to read' *David Starkey*

£9.99

978 07524 4386 7

If you are interested in purchasing other books published by Tempus, or in case you have difficulty finding
any Tempus books in your local bookshop, you can also place orders directly through our website:
www.tempus-publishing.com

TEMPUS – REVEALING HISTORY

Quacks Fakers and Charlatans in Medicine
ROY PORTER

'A delightful book' *The Daily Telegraph*
'Hugely entertaining' *BBC History Magazine*

£12.99   0 7524 2590 0

The Tudors
RICHARD REX

'Up-to-date, readable and reliable. The best introduction to England's most important dynasty' *David Starkey*

'Vivid, entertaining... quite simply the best short introduction' *Eamon Duffy*

'Told with enviable narrative skill... a delight for any reader' *THES*

£9.99   0 7524 3333 4

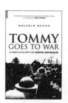

Okinawa 1945
GEORGE FEIFER

'A great book... Feifer's account of the three sides and their experiences far surpasses most books about war'
Stephen Ambrose

£17.99   0 7524 3324 5

Tommy Goes To War
MALCOLM BROWN

'A remarkably vivid and frank account of the British soldier in the trenches'
Max Arthur

'The fury, fear, mud, blood, boredom and bravery that made up life on the Western Front are vividly presented and illustrated'
The Sunday Telegraph

£12.99   0 7524 2980 4

The Kings & Queens of England
MARK ORMROD

'Of the numerous books on the kings and queens of England, this is the best'
Alison Weir

£9.99   0 7524 2598 6

The Covent Garden Ladies
Pimp General Jack & the Extraordinary Story of Harris's List
HALLIE RUBENHOLD

'Sex toys, porn... forget Ann Summers, Miss Love was at it 250 years ago' *The Times*
'Compelling' *The Independent on Sunday*
'Marvellous' *Leonie Frieda*
'Filthy' *The Guardian*

£9.99   0 7524 3739 9

Ace of Spies The True Story of Sidney Reilly
ANDREW COOK

'The most definitive biography of the spying ace yet written... both a compelling narrative and a myth-shattering *tour de force*'
Simon Sebag Montefiore

'The absolute last word on the subject' *Nigel West*
'Makes poor 007 look like a bit of a wuss'
The Mail on Sunday

£12.99   0 7524 2959 0

Sex Crimes
From Renaissance to Enlightenment
W.M. NAPHY

'Wonderfully scandalous' *Diarmaid MacCulloch*
'A model of pin-sharp scholarship' *The Guardian*

£10.99   0 7524 2977 9

If you are interested in purchasing other books published by Tempus, or in case you have difficulty finding any Tempus books in your local bookshop, you can also place orders directly through our website:
www.tempus-publishing.com

TEMPUS – REVEALING HISTORY

D-Day The First 72 Hours
WILLIAM F. BUCKINGHAM
'A compelling narrative' *The Observer*
A *BBC History Magazine* Book of the Year 2004
£9.99   0 7524 2842 X

The London Monster
Terror on the Streets in 1790
JAN BONDESON
'Gripping' *The Guardian*
'Excellent... monster-mania brought a reign of
terror to the ill-lit streets of the capital'
The Independent
£9.99   0 7524 3327 X

London
A Historical Companion
KENNETH PANTON
'A readable and reliable work of reference that
deserves a place on every Londoner's bookshelf'
Stephen Inwood
£20   0 7524 3434 9

M: MI5's First Spymaster
ANDREW COOK
'Serious spook history' *Andrew Roberts*
'Groundbreaking' *The Sunday Telegraph*
'Brilliantly researched' *Dame Stella Rimington*
£9.99   978 07524 3949 9

Agincourt
A New History
ANNE CURRY
'A highly distinguished and convincing account'
Christopher Hibbert
'A *tour de force*' *Alison Weir*
'*The* book on the battle' *Richard Holmes*
A *BBC History Magazine* Book of the Year 2005
£12.99   0 7524 3813 1

Battle of the Atlantic
MARC MILNER
'The most comprehensive short survey of the
U-boat battles' *Sir John Keegan*
'Some events are fortunate in their historian, none
more so than the Battle of the Atlantic. Marc
Milner is *the* historian of the Atlantic campaign... a
compelling narrative' *Andrew Lambert*
£12.99   0 7524 3332 6

The English Resistance
The Underground War Against the Normans
PETER REX
'An invaluable rehabilitation of an ignored
resistance movement' *The Sunday Times*
'Peter Rex's scholarship is remarkable'
The Sunday Express
£12.99   0 7524 3733 X

Elizabeth Wydeville: England's Slandered Queen
ARLENE OKERLUND
'A penetrating, thorough and wholly convincing
vindication of this unlucky queen'
Sarah Gristwood
'A gripping tale of lust, loss and tragedy'
Alison Weir
A *BBC History Magazine* Book of the Year 2005
£9.99   978 07524 3807 8

If you are interested in purchasing other books published by Tempus, or in case you have difficulty finding any
Tempus books in your local bookshop, you can also place orders directly through our website

www.tempus-publishing.com

TEMPUS – REVEALING HISTORY

Britannia's Empire
A Short History of the British Empire
BILL NASSON
'Crisp, economical and witty' *TLS*
'An excellent Introduction the subject' *THES*
£12.99   0 7524 3808 5

Born to be Gay
A History of Homosexuality
WILLIAM NAPHY
'Fascinating' *The Financial Times*
'Excellent' *Gay Times*
£9.99   0 7524 3694 5

Madmen
A Social History of Madhouses,
Mad-Doctors & Lunatics
ROY PORTER
'Fascinating'
The Observer
£12.99   0 7524 3730 5

William II
Rufus, the Red King
EMMA MASON
'A thoroughly new reappraisal of a much
maligned king. The dramatic story of his life is
told with great pace and insight'
John Gillingham
£25   0 7524 3528 0

To Kill Rasputin
The Life and Death of Grigori Rasputin
ANDREW COOK
'Andrew Cook is a brilliant investigative historian'
Andrew Roberts
'Astonishing' *The Daily Mail*
£9.99   0 7524 3906 5

Private 12768
Memoir of a Tommy
JOHN JACKSON
FOREWORD BY HEW STRACHAN
'A refreshing new perspective' *The Sunday Times*
'At last we have John Jackson's intensely
personal and heartfelt little book to remind us
there was a view of the Great War other than
Wilfred Owen's' *The Daily Mail*
£9.99   0 7524 3531 0

The Unwritten Order
Hitler's Role in the Final Solution
PETER LONGERICH
'Compelling' *Richard Evans*
'The finest account to date of the many twists
and turns in Adolf Hitler's anti-semitic obsession'
Richard Overy
£12.99   0 7524 3328 8

The Vikings
MAGNUS MAGNUSSON
'Serious, engaging history'
BBC History Magazine
£9.99   0 7524 2699 0

TEMPUS – REVEALING HISTORY

Freaks
JAN BONDESON

'Reveals how these tragic individuals triumphed over their terrible adversity' *The Daily Mail*
'Well written and superbly illustrated'
The Financial Times

£9.99   0 7524 3662 7

Bollywood
MIHIR BOSE

'Pure entertainment' *The Observer*
'Insightful and often hilarious' *The Sunday Times*
'Gripping' *The Daily Telegraph*

£9.99   978 07524 4382 9

King Arthur
CHRISTOPHER HIBBERT

'A pearl of biographers' *New Statesman*
£12.99   978 07524 3933 4

Arnhem
William Buckingham

'Reveals the reason why the daring attack failed'
The Daily Express

£10.99   0 7524 3187 0

Cleopatra
PATRICIA SOUTHERN

'In the absence of Cleopatra's memoirs Patricia Southern's commendably balanced biography will do very well'
The Sunday Telegraph

£9.99   978 07524 4336 2

The Prince In The Tower
MICHAEL HICKS

'The first time in ages that a publisher has sent me a book I actually want to read' *David Starkey*

£9.99   978 07524 4386 7

The Battle of Hastings 1066
M. K. LAWSON

'A *BBC History Magazine* book of the year 2003
'The definitive book on this famous battle'
The Journal of Military History

£12.99   978 07524 4177 1

Loos 1915
NICK LLOYD

'A revealing new account based on meticulous documentary research' *Corelli Barnett*
'Should fiinally consign Alan Clark's Farrago, *The Donkeys*, to the waste paperbasket'
Hew Strachan
'Plugs a yawning gap in the existing literature... this book will set the agenda for debate of the battle for years to come' *Gary Sheffield*

£25   0 7524 3937 5

If you are interested in purchasing other books published by Tempus, or in case you have difficulty finding any Tempus books in your local bookshop, you can also place orders directly through our website

www.tempus-publishing.com